Everyday Life:
THE CIVIL WAR

WALTER A. HAZEN

A GOOD YEAR BOOK™

GOOD YEAR BOOKS

Tucson, Arizona

Photo Credits

Front Cover: Civil War portraits courtesy of The Library of Congress, Bugle Fort St. Joseph Museum, Niles, MI. **Interior:** 2: Picture Collection/New York Public Library and Astor, Lenox and Tilden Foundations. 3: Picture Collection/New York Public Library and Astor, Lenox and Tilden Foundations. 4: Sophia Smith Collection, Smith College. 6: Harper's Weekly, April 27, 1861. 10: I.N. Phelps Stokes Collection/Prints Division/New York Public Library, Astor, Lenox and Tilden Foundations. 11: (bottom) International Harvester Company. 13, 18-20: The Library of Congress. 21: Mrs. Katherine McCook Knox. 26-29: The Library of Congress. 34: Chicago Historical Society. 35: (top & bottom) From the "Civil War-Master Index," photo copied by Michael Latil, © 1987 Time-Life Books, Inc., courtesy Tom Farish Collection, (center) from the "Civil War-Master Index," photo copied by Michael Latil, © 1987 Time-Life Books, Inc., courtesy Kean E. Wilcox. 37: (top) Chicago Historical Society, (bottom) from "Civil War-Master Index," photo copied by Michael Latil, © 1987 Time-Life Books, Inc., courtesy Kean E. Wilcox. 42: Harper's Weekly, July 20 1861/The Newberry Library, Chicago. 43: Museum of the Confederacy. 44: New York Historical Society. 45: Harper's Weekly, December 31, 1864. 50: The Library of Congress. 51: (top) The Library of Congress, (bottom) Frank Leslie's Illustrated Newspaper, August 31, 1861. 52: Chicago Historical Society. 53: Western Reserve Historical Society. 58: CORBIS/Bettmann. 54: Culver Pictures, Inc. 60: Boston Public Library. 61: The Library of Congress. 66: Massachusetts Historical Society. 67: Chicago Historical Society. 68: The Library of Congress. 69: The Library of Congress. 74: (top) Winslow Homer, "The Letter From Home," Philadelphia Museum of Art, The Harrison Fund. 75: Courtesy of the American Red Cross. 76: The Library of Congress. 77: Chicago Historical Society. 81: (top) The Library of Congress, (bottom) Frank Leslie's Illustrated Newspaper, May 6, 1865. 82: New York Historical Society. 83: U.S. Signal Corps Photo/National Archives. 84: CORBIS/Bettmann.

Dedication

To Martha, Jordan, and Allison

Acknowledgments

Grateful acknowledgment is extended to my editor, Laura Strom, who has guided me through several books in Good Year's "Everyday Life" series. Without her advice and support, this book would not have been possible.

I would also like to thank Roberta Dempsey, Editorial Director at Good Year, for giving me the opportunity to be a part of such an exciting project. Her support and condidence in me is likewise appreciated.

Everyday Life: The Civil War contains lessons and activities that reinforce and develop skills defined by the National Council of Social Studies as appropriate for students in the upper elementary and middle school grades. These lessons and activities focus on, but are not limited to, (1) the causes of the Civil War; (2) the course of the war and its effects on the American people; and (3) the plans of reconstruction that followed the war. In addition to social studies, some activities at the ends of the various chapters deal with such skills as writing, critical thinking, and math. All activities, of course, relate to the Civil War. See www.goodyearbooks.com for information on how lessons correlate to specific standards.

Good Year Books

Our titles are available for most basic curriculum subjects plus many enrichment areas. For information on other Good Year Books and to place orders, contact your local bookseller or educational dealer, or visit our website at www.goodyearbooks.com. For a complete catalog, please contact:

Good Year Books
PO Box 91858
Tucson, AZ 85752-1858
www.goodyearbooks.com

Design: Ronan Design
Silhouette Drawings: Joe Rogers

A GOOD YEAR BOOK™

Table of Contents

Table of Contents *continued*

From *Everyday Life: The Civil War* ©1999 Good Year Books.

Introduction

Everyday Life: The Civil War is exactly what the title implies. It is a survey of what everyday life was like during a most trying time in our nation's history. Battles are mentioned in connection with other events, but, except for the First Battle of Bull Run, they are not the focus of the book.

In *Everyday Life: The Civil War,* you will follow young Union and Confederate soldiers through training and on to the hardships and boredom of camp life. You will accompany them as they go into battle for the first time and share their feelings and apprehensions. All the while, you will learn how they dressed, how they were equipped, and what they ate. You will also learn about innovations, or changes, in warfare that impacted the daily lives of these young men.

In *Everyday Life: The Civil War,* you will come to appreciate the role played by women in the war —not only on the home fronts, but also in the hospitals and on the battlefields. You will learn that a number of women served as spies, and some even disguised themselves as men and fought as soldiers. Also, you will learn of the contributions of African American soldiers, without whose services the Union might not have won the war.

The Civil War was unlike any other war in our nation's history. It pitted American against American and was characterized by unbelievable suffering and slaughter. In *Everyday Life: The Civil War,* you will learn about conditions in field hospitals and prisons, as well as about the hardships endured by the civilian populations of both the North and the South.

A variety of activities following each chapter of the book should make learning with *Everyday Life: The Civil War* an interesting and rewarding experience.

Walter A. Hazen

CHAPTER I

Background and Causes

On August 20, 1619, a Dutch merchant ship docked at Jamestown, Virginia, with a most unusual cargo. Aboard were the first twenty black Africans to be brought to the shores of North America. Although these unfortunate captives were sold to English colonists as indentured servants and not as slaves, an era in history had begun. All future shipments of blacks to America were sold as slaves, most of them in the Southern colonies. The institution of slavery in America had begun, and it would continue for almost 250 years. It did not end until the Union (Northerners) defeated the Confederacy (Southerners) in the Civil War.

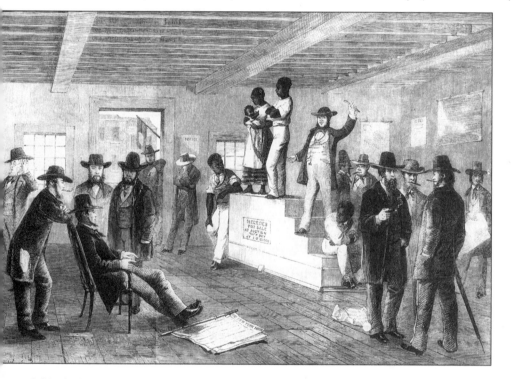

The number of African slaves brought to the English colonies steadily increased after 1619. By the time of the American Revolution, there were about 500,000 spread throughout the thirteen colonies. The vast majority of these were in the South. The South's warm climate and rich soil encouraged the establishment of large farms and plantations. Although slaves could be found in every colony, slavery never became firmly established in the North. This was particularly true in New England, where rocky soil and a harsh climate tended to keep farms small. There was also strong antislavery feeling among Northern colonists. As a result, most slaves in the North were granted their freedom by the end of the 18th century. Vermont abolished slavery altogether in 1777, followed by Massachusetts six years later. By 1799 Pennsylvania, Rhode Island, Connecticut, and New York had decided to ban

A black slave family being sold at public auction. Sometimes, in heart-rending scenes, family members were sold separately.

From *Everyday Life: The Civil War* ©1999 Good Year Books.

slavery on a gradual basis. Then, in 1808, the United States Congress prohibited the further importation of slaves into the country.

The end of the slave trade, however, had no effect on the slaves already in the United States. By 1800 their numbers had swelled to 1,500,000. Again, most of these were in the Southern colonies, where large numbers of laborers were needed to work on plantations. But soon a real sectional conflict began to develop between the North and the South regarding the spread of slavery to the western territories.

The first big argument over slavery took place in 1819. In that year Missouri asked to be admitted to the Union as a slave state. Missouri was part of the vast area of land known as the Louisiana Territory that the United States had purchased from France in 1803. Many of the settlers who had moved there were from the South and owned slaves. But Missouri's request was turned down by Congress, where the House of Representatives was controlled by Northern congressmen.

Shortly afterward, Maine applied for admission as a free state. Since there were eleven slave states and eleven free states, its admission in turn was blocked by Southerners in the Senate. The Compromise of 1820 settled the issue. (A compromise is an agreement in which each side gives in on certain things.) Missouri came into the Union as a slave state and Maine as a free state. A line drawn westward on a map of the Louisiana Territory provided that slavery would be forbidden in all new states formed north of the line. All future states created south of the line would be admitted as slave states.

The Compromise of 1820 worked well for a while. Then the issue of slavery's expansion rose again. From 1846 to 1848 the United States fought and won a war with Mexico. As a result, another huge area of land was added to our nation's boundaries. It included California and what would become the territories of Utah and New Mexico. Tensions flared once more. The people of California asked to be admitted to the Union as a free state. This upset Southerners, who saw the balance of power swinging in favor of the free states.

Another compromise was reached. California was admitted as a free state, while settlers in the territories of New Mexico and Utah could decide the slavery issue themselves. Also, a strong Fugitive Slave Law was passed

A handbill announcing the sale of three slaves along with livestock and other property. Such posters were common sights in cities where slave auctions were held.

requiring that runaway slaves be returned to their owners in the South. This agreement satisfied both sections of the country until violence broke out in the territory of Kansas a few years later.

In 1854 Congress passed the Kansas-Nebraska Act. This new law set aside the Missouri Compromise of 1820, which had forbidden slavery north of a line that now included the territories of Kansas and Nebraska. The Kansas-Nebraska Act left it to the people of the two territories to decide themselves whether they wanted to be slave or free. Settlers from both the North and the South quickly rushed in. Those from the North wanted Kansas and Nebraska to be free territories. Those from the South wanted slavery established. The two sides came to

Harriet Tubman (far left) poses with a group of slaves she led to freedom.

blows in Kansas. A bloody war erupted that continued for three years and cost more than 200 lives. It was finally put down by U.S. troops in 1857.

Other factors helped bring on the Civil War. Nearly all were associated with slavery. A number of slave uprisings took place in the South before 1861, and Southerners blamed these on the encouragement of Northern abolitionists. Abolitionists were people who felt that slavery was wrong and wanted to see it ended. Some abolitionists preached violence; others sought to change things through speeches and writings. Many risked their lives to help slaves escape to the North and to Canada by way of the Underground Railroad.

The Underground Railroad was no railroad at all. It was a series of hiding places and escape routes where runaway slaves were led to freedom by "conductors." Conductors were abolitionists familiar with routes and with houses and barns where slaves could stop to rest and get food. Some conductors were white; others were black. Probably the most famous was Harriet Tubman, who had escaped from slavery herself. She returned to the

From *Everyday Life: The Civil War* © 1999 Good Year Books.

South some nineteen times and led more than three hundred slaves to safety and freedom.

The activities of the abolitionists and the Underground Railroad brought the North and the South ever closer to war. Southern planters were angered that they were losing valuable property (slaves) in record numbers. They asked that the North enforce the Fugitive Slave Law by returning runaway slaves. Some were returned but many were not.

You are probably familiar with the expression "The pen is mightier than the sword." This means that the written word often gets quicker results than an uprising or a war. This was true with regard to the influence of abolitionist newspapers in the North that called for an end to slavery. Because of such newspapers, many white people became convinced that slavery was wrong and should be ended.

Even more convincing was a book that appeared in 1852. That book was Harriet Beecher Stowe's *Uncle Tom's Cabin*. It dealt with the evils of the slave system and the way in which slaves were treated. In the book a cruel overseer named Simon Legree whipped an old slave named Uncle Tom so viciously that he died. Northerners accepted the book as a true picture of slavery in the South, and more people joined the cause of the abolitionists.

Southerners objected strongly to *Uncle Tom's Cabin*. They maintained that the Bible approved of slavery. They said that most slaves were better off than factory workers in the North. Did all slaves in the South suffer in the manner of Uncle Tom? Or were most slaves valued and treated kindly by their masters? The truth lies somewhere in between. Some slave owners, to be sure, were cruel tyrants who punished their slaves mercilessly. But others were kind and sincerely concerned with the welfare of the slaves in their charge.

Another incident occurred in 1857 that created more dissension between the North and the South. Dred Scott, the slave of an army doctor named John Emerson, was taken from Missouri, a slave state, to Illinois, a free state. When he later returned to Missouri with his owner, he declared that he was a free man because he had lived for a while in a free state. He took his case all the way to the Supreme Court. He lost. The Court ruled that a slave was property and therefore had no rights. It further stated that it had no power to take away a person's property. What the Court was really saying was that it could not keep slavery out of new states when they were formed.

The Dred Scott case was hailed in the South and scorned in the North. It caused many Northerners to join the Republican Party, a political organization

Confederate guns fire on Fort Sumter, South Carolina, starting the Civil War. From Harper's Pictorial History of the Civil War.

that had been formed only three years before (in 1854). The Republican Party was organized several months after the Kansas-Nebraska Act was passed by Congress. In fact it was organized in protest to the Act. The Republican Party took up the cause of abolition and made it an important part of their program.

There was one cause of the Civil War that had nothing to do with slavery. That was a disagreement over tariffs. A tariff is a tax on foreign goods coming into a country. The North, being primarily a manufacturing region, naturally favored a high protective tariff. A tariff would increase the costs of products from other countries and allow goods made in American factories to be sold at a cheaper price. The South, an agricultural society that bought many of its products from England, strongly objected to the tariff.

Conditions grew even worse in 1859. By then people who were called radical abolitionists were demanding an immediate end to slavery. John Brown, who was a radical abolitionist, led a group of about twenty followers, including three of his sons, on a raid of the federal arsenal at Harpers Ferry, Virginia. His plan was to seize guns, arm the slaves, and bring about a slave rebellion. The rebellion never took place. Brown was captured shortly after the attempt and hanged six weeks later.

When Abraham Lincoln was elected President in 1860, thirteen states seceded from the United States and formed the Confederate States of America. On April 12, 1861, Confederate guns fired on Fort Sumter, South Carolina. The Civil War had begun. It would not end for four long, bloody years.

From *Everyday Life: The Civil War* ©1999 Good Year Books.

Name _____ Date _____

Write a Letter About the Evils of Slavery

Pretend that you are a strong opponent of slavery and are living in the North in the years before the Civil War. Also imagine that one of your cousins is a member of a slaveholding family that owns a large tobacco plantation somewhere in the South.

Write a letter to your cousin giving reasons why you think slavery is wrong and should be abolished.

Date_____

Dear _____,

_____

_____

_____

_____

_____

_____

_____

_____

_____

_____

_____

_____

_____

_____

_____

_____

_____

_____

Your cousin,

_____

Name _____ Date _____

Create a Graph of Your Own

You have learned that the first Africans were brought to these shores in 1619. Although only twenty arrived on that initial ship, the number of slaves in America increased rapidly over the next 200-plus years.

Using the dates and figures listed, create a line or bar graph in the space provided. At the bottom of your graph, also create several word problems associated with it. Ask a classmate to solve the problems.

NUMBER OF SLAVES

4,000,000				
3,500,000				
3,000,000				
2,500,000				
2,000,000				
1,500,000				
1,000,000				
500,000				
0				

500,000	700,000	1,500,000	3,200,000	400,000,000
1776	1790	1800	1850	1860

YEAR

_____

_____

_____

_____

_____

_____

_____

_____

From *Everyday Life: The Civil War* ©1999 Good Year Books.

Name _____ Date _____

Name Those States and Territories

At the time of the Civil War, the United States consisted of thirty-four states and eight territories, if Indian Territory is included among the latter. Nineteen states made up the Union when the war began. Eleven states seceded and formed the Confederacy. Four border states remained loyal to the North. Seven of the eight territories fought on the side of the Union.

Find these states and territories on a map of the United States as it was in 1861. Consult an American History text or look under Civil War in an encyclopedia. Then list each under the proper heading.

The Union States:

_____
_____
_____
_____
_____
_____
_____
_____
_____
_____
_____
_____
_____
_____
_____
_____
_____
_____
_____

The Border States:

_____
_____
_____
_____

The Confederate States:

_____
_____
_____
_____
_____
_____
_____
_____
_____
_____
_____

Territories That Fought for the Union

_____
_____
_____
_____
_____
_____
_____

CHAPTER 2

Advantages of the North and the South

If you were to list the advantages of the North side by side with those of the South, you might wonder how the Civil War continued for four long years. In sheer numbers the North had more of everything. They had more people, more guns, and more money. Why, then, did the Union not achieve a quick victory? This question will be answered after the strengths of both sides are pointed out.

The Union enjoyed a huge advantage in population. There were 22,000,000 people living in the North in 1861. The Confederacy could count only 9,000,000, and more than one-third of these were slaves. A steady flow of immigrants from Europe provided the Union with a tremendous amount of manpower to run the factories and fill the ranks of the army. Over 2,000,000 men served in the Union armies during the war. Only

An 1850 aerial illustration of Utica, NY, showing a large amount of industry.

about half that number fought in the armies of the Confederacy.

The North also had an advantage in manufacturing. There were about 110,000 factories in the North, compared to 18,000 in the South. Of the 31,000 miles of railroad track in the United States, 22,000 were in the North. In 1860 the states of New York and Pennsylvania had each produced twice as many goods as the entire Confederacy combined. Nearly all war supplies were made in the North. Northern states produced 97 percent of the nation's firearms and 96 percent of the railway equipment. The South, on the other hand, had to look elsewhere for its supplies. Most of its guns, medicines, and ammunition were purchased from foreign countries.

The North did face one disadvantage at the start of the war. Its army numbered only 17,000 men, and most of these were stationed at remote forts on the frontier. Further, many of its most capable officers resigned and joined

From *Everyday Life: The Civil War* ©1999 Good Year Books.

the Confederate army. In terms of strength and preparedness, the Union army was not ready to go into battle in 1861.

The South enjoyed certain advantages as well. Not the least of these was the spirit and confidence of its people. After Fort Sumter, young volunteers hurried to enlist in the state militias. Most Southerners believed that "one good Southern boy could whip any ten Yankee [Northern] clerks and shopkeepers hands down." Southerners, after all, had been introduced to the horse and firearms early in childhood. Surely they were better than their Northern counterparts at such "manly pursuits."

Confederate soldiers were also fighting on familiar ground. They knew the terrain well and had shorter supply and communication lines. And since most battles were fought on Southern soil, the Confederate army seldom had to worry about fighting behind enemy lines.

Slaves at work on a plantation, carrying cotton bundles on their heads.

Perhaps the greatest advantage held by the South was that it could fight a defensive war. It did not have to invade and conquer the North. And it did not have to win. The South could lose battle after battle and still achieve its goal. All it needed to do was to hold out long enough to make the North grow tired of fighting and give up the struggle.

A final advantage of the South lay in military leadership. The Confederacy had the more able generals at the start of the war. One of the best was Robert E. Lee. President Lincoln had asked Lee to command the Union armies when the war started, but he declined. Lee was no supporter of slavery, but he could not bring himself to fight against his home state of Virginia. Other key military leaders were Generals Thomas "Stonewall" Jackson and Pierre G. T. Beauregard. These officers had graduated from the United States Military Academy in West Point, New York. They knew well how to command troops.

But it is obvious, from the standpoint of manpower and industrial strength, that the advantages of the North far outweighed those of the South.

A close look at the cotton plant, which made slavery an institution in the South and indirectly helped bring on the Civil War.

Why then, as was asked earlier, did the war last so long?

Several reasons explain the duration of the conflict. First, neither side was prepared to carry on a full-scale war. Not only was the small Union army scattered throughout the West, but its navy was assigned to different places around the world. Of fifty-three active ships in 1861, eleven were captured by the Confederacy after Fort Sumter. That left only forty-two ships to blockade the South in hopes of preventing needed supplies from coming in. Forty-two ships were not enough to carry out the task.

The South was in even worse shape. It had no regular army as did the North. Each state had a small militia made up largely of farmers. Although Confederate President Jefferson Davis's call for 100,000 volunteers was enthusiastically answered, these volunteers were raw recruits. They needed to be trained and disciplined to become soldiers. Training inexperienced troops takes time.

Like Jefferson Davis in the South, President Lincoln also asked for volunteers to fill the Union army. Since men did not volunteer fast enough, the government offered a bounty (gift of money) to all who would. Some dishonest enlistees took advantage of the situation and became bounty jumpers. This meant they would enlist in one town, collect their money, and then run away to another town and enlist there, again collecting their bounty. They continued moving from place to place until some grew quite rich.

Both the Union and the Confederacy eventually resorted to the draft. The South began to draft all men between the ages of eighteen and thirty-five in 1862. One year later, the North started calling up anyone between twenty and forty-five. Both sides offered a way out of service. A Southerner who owned twenty or more slaves did not have to fight. Others were able to pay a substitute to take their place. A Northerner with $300 also could pay a fee and be excused. Because men with money could buy their way out fighting, some people referred to the war as a "rich man's war and a poor man's fight."

A second reason why the Civil War lasted so long had to do with the seasons. In general, the opposing armies did little fighting in the winter

Union and Confederate Resources 1861

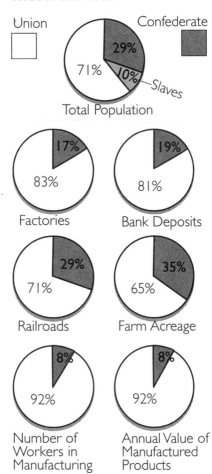

Union ☐   Confederate ◼

29% / 71% / 10% — Slaves
Total Population

17% / 83%
Factories

19% / 81%
Bank Deposits

29% / 71%
Railroads

35% / 65%
Farm Acreage

8% / 92%
Number of Workers in Manufacturing

8% / 92%
Annual Value of Manufactured Products

A chart comparing the resources of the North and the South at the beginning of the war. The Union had a clear advantage in every area.

From *Everyday Life: The Civil War* ©1999 Good Year Books.

months, when cold weather and mud made the movement of guns and wagons difficult. Therefore, while the war lasted four years, actual fighting took place only during a portion of each of those years.

A final reason for the length of the war concerned the number of soldiers required by the Union armies. Because the South was fighting a defensive war, it could make do with far fewer troops. But the North needed soldiers to guard and hold every important place it conquered. It also needed soldiers to care for and feed thousands of freed or runaway slaves who came under its protection. Therefore, the North's tremendous advantage in numbers was offset somewhat by the manner in which it had to use many of its troops.

Men in both the North and the South who had money could avoid fighting by hiring a substitute to go in their places. Many did.

Who were these troops who filled the ranks of both armies? They came from all walks of life and all kinds of families. Often families were divided in their allegiance to one side or the other. Even the powerful were not spared the agony of seeing some members fight for the North and others for the South. President Lincoln's wife, Mary Todd Lincoln, had three brothers and a brother-in-law who were officers in the Confederate Army. Thus, the President himself had four brothers-in-law who fought for the South.

It was especially painful for families who lived in the border states. The border states were the states situated between the two sections of the country. There were eight: Virginia, Tennessee, North Carolina, Arkansas, Delaware, Missouri, Kentucky, and Maryland. Virginia, Tennessee, North Carolina, and Arkansas joined the Confederacy. Delaware, Missouri, Kentucky, and Maryland remained loyal to the Union. West Virginia broke away from Virginia in 1863 and also sided with the North.

In the border states, families were split apart by the war. One brother might enlist to fight for the North and another for the South. Cousin fought against cousin and uncle against nephew. And in both Northern and Southern states there were men who marched off to fight for the other side. Some soldiers fought for both. They would become disillusioned with one army and end up fighting for the other. What a strange war!

The war was even more strange considering the number of boys who participated. Many were as young as eight or nine. Their story will be told in Chapter 5.

Name _____ Date _____

Reading Between the Lines

To *infer* means to reach an opinion or come to a conclusion after thinking about something you have read. Some people call it "reading between the lines."

At right are factual statements from Chapter 2 dealing with the advantages of the North and the South. Read each and below write what you think the statement is inferring.

1. Fact: The Union had more soldiers and guns at the beginning of the war.

   Inference: _____
   _____

2. Fact: Some of the best officers in the United States Army resigned to join the Confederacy.

   Inference: _____
   _____

3. Fact: Many Southerners believed "one good Southern boy could whip any ten Yankee clerks and shopkeepers hands down any day."

   Inference: _____
   _____

4. Fact: At the beginning of the war, most of the United States Army was scattered at military posts throughout the West.

   Inference: _____
   _____

5. Fact: The South needed only to fight a defensive war.

   Inference: _____

6. Fact: Armies years ago often did not fight battles during the winter months.

   Inference: _____

7. Fact: Family members and relatives sometimes fought against each other in the Civil War.

   Inference: _____
   _____

From *Everyday Life: The Civil War* ©1999 Good Year Books.

Name _____ Date _____

Help Thomas Get to Minnesota

Thomas is a 19-year-old laborer in Lake Charles, Louisiana, who does not support slavery. Certain that a war is about to break out between the North and the South, he desires to travel to Minnesota to offer his services as a soldier. He hopes that he can enlist in the same regiment as his brother Paul, who is a sergeant there in the United States Army.

Help Thomas find his way north by filling in the blanks in the sentences below.

1. If Thomas drew a line from Lake Charles, Louisiana, to Minnesota, he would pass in order through the states of _____, _____, and _____.

2. The capitals of the above three states are _____, _____, and _____.

3. Traveling north, Thomas would pass through the _____ Mountains, which form the southern edge of the Ozarks.

4. Thomas decides to stop over at Missouri's capital, which is located on the _____ River.

5. After leaving the capital of Missouri, Thomas decides to travel to Kansas City. In which direction must he travel?
   _____

6. From Kansas City Thomas makes plans to go to Des Moines, Iowa. To do so, he would travel in which direction?
   _____

7. While in Des Moines, Thomas notices on his map that the states of _____ and _____ border Iowa on the east, while the territories of _____ and _____ border it on the west.

8. Crossing the Minnesota state line, Thomas strikes out for _____, the state's capital.

9. From Minnesota's capital, Thomas must head _____ (which direction?) to Duluth, where he hopes to meet his brother and inquire about enlisting in the army.

CHAPTER 3

Setting the Stage

So many wars in history have begun amid an almost carnival-like atmosphere. The Civil War was no exception. In both the North and the South, troops were cheered by wives, sweethearts, children, and older citizens as they proudly marched through the streets of their home towns on the way to battle. Bands played and flags waved. Everyone expected the war to last only a few weeks, after which their loved ones would return as conquering heroes. No one would get hurt and everyone would be awarded a chestful of medals—or so it seemed to people completely ignorant of the horrible realities of war.

So confident were the people of Washington, D.C., of a quick Union victory that they hurried out to watch the first important battle. They came in fancy carriages with their picnic baskets in hand, ready for an afternoon of fun and entertainment. Little did they realize the catastrophe that would unfold.

A Union officer says goodbye to his wife and parents as the Army of Cumberland marches past his home.

By midsummer of 1861, although the North and South had been at war for two months, little action had taken place. There had been a few skirmishes, or minor battles, but nothing of consequence. This changed in July when the Confederate government decided to move its capital from Montgomery, Alabama, to Richmond, Virginia. The Confederate Congress was scheduled to meet in Richmond on July 20. With Richmond little more than 100 miles from Washington, D.C., Northern newspapers called for immediate action. They argued that a march on the Southern city would prevent the Rebel Congress from meeting and bring a quick end to the war.

About thirty miles from Washington was the small town of Manassas, Virginia. Manassas was an important railroad junction from which the North could launch an attack in the direction of Richmond. It was also an ideal jumping-off place for a Confederate attack on Washington, if the South were

From *Everyday Life: The Civil War* ©1999 Good Year Books.

so inclined. Here, on July 21, 1861, at a small stream called Bull Run, the first major battle of the Civil War was fought.

Although the morning of July 21 was hot and sultry in Washington, the city was a beehive of activity. News of the upcoming attack had spread rapidly. Thousands of people made hasty plans to ride out to watch the Southern troops get the licking they justly deserved. Not all were ordinary citizens. At least six senators and an undetermined number of congressmen were among them. They left Washington on horseback and in various types of carriages. With them were pretty ladies in fancy gowns and even fancier hats. And, as previously mentioned, they took their picnic baskets with them.

There seemed no cause for alarm that Sunday morning in Washington. President Lincoln went to church as usual, and in the afternoon he took his customary carriage ride. Seventy-five-year-old General Winfield Scott, the Commander of the Union Army, was so confident of victory that he spent the better part of the day napping. No one in their wildest dreams could imagine that anything would go wrong at Manassas.

All did go well for the Northerners at first. The 35,000 Union troops under General Irvin McDowell almost put the Confederates to flight. Although McDowell's soldiers were mostly inexperienced, they fought

Scene from the First Battle of Bull Run, July 21, 1861. A smashing Confederate victory, it proved that the war would not be a short one.

admirably against the equally inexperienced Southern troops. Their performance, in fact, prompted General McDowell to wire General Scott that victory could be expected at any minute. The old general read the message and went back to sleep. President Lincoln left the White House for his carriage ride, thinking all was well.

Matters quickly changed in the afternoon. Ten thousand additional Southern troops arrived at Manassas by railroad and joined the battle. Their appearance turned the tide in favor of the South. Their blood-curdling "Rebel yell" so frightened the green Northern

troops that the latter turned and ran. What started as a retreat soon turned into a panic-stricken rout. The boys in blue threw away their guns and other equipment and dashed off for safety in the direction of Washington.

Many bystanders witnessed the wild retreat to the nation's capital. Some were reporters, others congressmen or citizens from the city. Many tried to prevent the Union soldiers from running away. Several congressmen grabbed discarded rifles and threatened to shoot anyone who did not stop. They shouted at retreating soldiers and called them cowards and names much worse. But nothing could slow down the frantic mass of soldiers fleeing along the roads and through the woods. And for miles on the route to Washington, the roadway was littered with hats, blankets, coats, guns, canteens, provisions, and turned-over carts and wagons.

Horrifying scenes greeted all those who fled along the escape route. Bleeding horses still attached to carts and guns gnawed at their sides in agony

as they lay dying in ditches. Wounded men lay by the side of the road, pleading not to be left behind. One cavalry officer was seen riding his charging horse over the body of a man with no legs who had crawled into the center of the road. Crazed horses pulling artillery pieces trampled over others. It was a scene that would haunt survivors for years to come.

Even the picnickers joined in the flight to Washington. Before the battle began, they had spread their picnic blankets on the ground on a hill overlooking Bull Run Creek to watch

Two black Union soldiers take aim at their Confederate foe. Black troops began to see action in the Union Army after 1863.

the day's events. When the frenzied rout began, they left their fine foods and wines to the ants and the victorious Rebels, and beat a hasty retreat back to the capital. Their presence clogged the roads and added even more chaos to the Union retreat.

One amusing story emerged from all the chaos and confusion. That story concerned a long-legged legislator who afterwards was referred to as "the Flying Congressman."

From *Everyday Life: The Civil War* ©1999 Good Year Books.

As the rout began, a very tall congressman in a long-tailed coat and wearing a high silk hat was seen leading the entire pack back to Washington. He was ahead of everyone and everything, even the horses and carriages. Witnesses later swore that he cleared ditches and gullies in a single leap. Once he was seen jumping a six-foot fence with plenty of room to spare. He lost his expensive hat while clearing the fence, but he did not stop to retrieve it. When he arrived panting in the streets of the city, none other than President Lincoln came out to meet and to scold him. The President was supposed to have dryly congratulated him on "winning the race."

A drizzling rain fell on Washington the Monday after the Bull Run disaster. All that day, dazed Union soldiers crossed the Potomac River into the city. They had no idea where to go or what to do. They did not even know where army headquarters were. They were tired, hungry, and completely confused. Kindhearted ladies of Washington cooked soups and stews and served the men from large wash boilers. Afterward, what remained of a once-confident army fell asleep on lawns, porches, and sidewalks.

Posters like this one of "Miss Liberty" were designed to stir patriotism in both the North and the South.

You may wonder why the victorious Southern troops did not pursue the fleeing Union Army. You may also wonder why they did not take advantage of the situation and possibly even march on Washington. The answer was that they were shocked into inactivity. No one was prepared for what they saw in the aftermath of the battle. Bodies were everywhere. Many had no arms or legs and some had no heads. Terrible new weapons used for the first time in warfare had created a scene of horror. Surviving soldiers could only stare in disbelief at what they saw. As a result, few were inclined to chase after a defeated enemy.

The First Battle of Bull Run brought home several realities of war to both the North and the South. First, the battle showed that war was no game or picnic. People actually got killed. The Union forces counted 460 dead, more than 1,100 wounded, and more than 1,300 missing. Confederate losses were put at 378 killed, almost 1,500 wounded, and 30 missing.

Second, Bull Run proved that the war would not end quickly. Instead of being over in a day as the North had expected, it would drag on for four years. Gone in one hot, summer afternoon were all ideas of immediate glory and a quick victory.

Name _____ Date _____

Write a Story for *The Bull Run Bulletin*

Pretend that you are a roving reporter for *The Bull Run Bulletin* and that you have just witnessed— at a safe distance— the First Battle of Bull Run. Your assignment is to write a story on the outcome of the battle.

On the lines provided, write the lead paragraph to your story. Be sure to include answers to the five "W" questions (Who? What? When? Where? and Why?) that are characteristic of a good lead paragraph. The headlines have been written for you.

The Bull Run Bulletin
★ ★ ★ ★ ☆ **July 22, 1861** ☆ ★ ★ ★ ★

Yanks Routed at Creek
Huge Victory for the South

_____

_____

_____

_____

_____

_____

_____

_____

_____

_____

_____

_____

_____

_____

_____

_____

_____

_____

_____

From *Everyday Life: The Civil War* ©1999 Good Year Books.

Name _____ Date _____

Use Context Clues to Complete Sentences

The meaning of a word often depends on its context, or the way it is used in a sentence. You can use context clues to help you better understand what you have read. With this in mind, use the words from the word box to fill in the blanks in the sentences telling the story of General Stonewall Jackson.

acquired

amidst

attempted

deeply

encouraging

famous

inspired

rally

stepped

stone

suffering

teased

thin

unlikely

unpopular

You have probably heard of that _____ Confederate general, Thomas Jonathan "Stonewall" Jackson. But do you know how he _____ his nickname?

General Jackson was a most _____ candidate to be called "Stonewall." In appearance, he was small and _____. He was a hypochondriac who imagined himself _____ from all kinds of illnesses, which he _____ to treat with an assortment of foods and medicines. He was also a _____ religious man who spent hours each day in prayer.

Before the Civil War, Jackson was an _____ professor at the Virginia Military Institute at Lexington, Virginia. He was constantly _____ by students because of his ways and his small size. But when he _____ onto the battlefield, a strange transformation took place. He became an _____ leader and one of the most able commanders in the Confederate Army.

At Bull Run, Jackson won the respect of everyone by _____ his brigade to hold an important hill against overwhelming odds. Another Southern general, trying to _____ his own troops, saw Jackson standing _____ the smoke and the din and shouted: "There stands Jackson like a _____ wall."

Thereafter, Thomas Jonathan Jackson was "Stonewall" to all who knew him.

From Everyday Life: The Civil War ©1999 Good Year Books.

Name _____ Date _____

Solve Some Bull Run Word Problems

Use the spaces provided to answer these word problems.

1. A distinguished senator left Washington by carriage at 5 A.M. His destination was Bull Run, about 30 miles to the southwest. If he arrived on the scene at 10 A.M., what speed had he averaged in getting there?

    _____ miles per hour

2. When the wild retreat back to Washington began, the same distinguished senator abandoned his carriage, mounted his horse bareback, and sped off in a cloud of dust. If he left Bull Run at 4:30 P.M. and his horse galloped at a speed of 15 miles per hour, what time did he arrive back in Washington?

    _____ P.M.

3. The total number of soldiers killed at Bull Run was 838. Of these, 460 were Union. What percentage were Confederate? (Round your answer.)

    _____ %

4. Approximately 70,000 troops participated in the First Battle of Bull Run. Total casualties—killed, wounded, and missing in action—came to 6.4%. How many casualties were there all together?

    _____ casualties

From *Everyday Life: The Civil War* ©1999 Good Year Books.

Name _____ Date _____

Create a Dialogue Between Two Soldiers

You have learned that the Union Army suffered an unexpected and stunning defeat at Bull Run on July 21, 1861. As the exhausted soldiers made their way back to Washington and collapsed on sidewalks and lawns, conversations among them surely took place concerning the events of the day.

On the lines at right, create a dialogue between two Union soldiers in which they discuss the battle and reveal their feelings about the realities of war.

_____

_____

_____

_____

_____

_____

_____

_____

_____

_____

_____

_____

_____

_____

_____

_____

_____

_____

_____

_____

_____

_____

CHAPTER 4

The Leaders

What was to become of the United States after 1861 lay largely in the hands of four men. Two held the title of President. Two were the commanders of their respective armies in the North and South. These men were Abraham Lincoln, Jefferson Davis, Ulysses S. Grant, and Robert E. Lee.

Abraham Lincoln was the sixteenth President of the United States. He served his nation at a time that severely tested his courage and leadership. Because of his wisdom and his compassion for people, many consider him one of the greatest leaders of all time.

Lincoln was born in a log cabin in Kentucky in 1809. When he was seven, he moved with his family to Indiana. There he lived in a half-faced camp (a crude, three-sided shelter) until his father completed building a cabin. As Abe grew older, he worked hard helping his father. He split rails, planted crops, and performed numerous other chores.

Young Abe had a passion for reading. He read everything he could lay his hands on, often walking miles to borrow a book. He once commented that he had borrowed and read every book within a fifty-mile radius. He carried books with him into the fields and read at night by the light from the fireplace.

At Antietam, President Lincoln (left) meeting with General George McClellan, commander of the Union Armies.

Abraham Lincoln was popular with the people in his region of Indiana. As he grew into a young man, he became an excellent speaker and storyteller. He was also known for his strength and athletic ability. He could out-lift all competitors in a barrel-lifting contest and outdistance all runners in a foot race. At six-feet, four-inches tall and 180 pounds, he was no pushover at wrestling, either.

From *Everyday Life: The Civil War* ©1999 Good Year Books.

When Lincoln was twenty-one, he moved with his father to Illinois. (His mother had died when he was eight.) There he worked at odd jobs, including a stint as a clerk in a general store. It was while working in the store that he won his nickname, "Honest Abe."

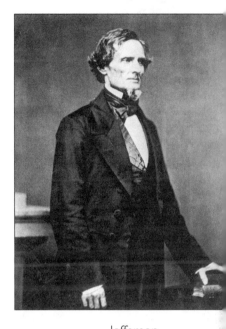

One day a lady came into the store and purchased several items. When she left, Lincoln realized he had not given her the correct change. Did he simply pocket the money and forget the whole thing? No. He walked three miles to give his surprised customer what was due her: six cents!

Lincoln went on to become a lawyer and an Illinois state legislator. In 1846 he was elected to the U.S. House of Representatives, where he served one term. Twelve years later, he ran for the U.S. Senate. Although he lost the senatorial election to Stephen A. Douglas, he gained national attention by debating his opponent on the issue of slavery. Lincoln believed that "no house divided against itself could stand"; that is, that no nation could survive half slave and half free. Two years later, he was named the Republican Party's candidate for President. He was elected and entered the White House on March 4, 1861. One month later, the Civil War broke out.

Jefferson Davis, President of the Confederate States of America. From a photograph by Mathew Brady.

As President, Lincoln felt it was his duty to preserve the Union. No state, he said, could simply quit the United States of America and strike out on its own. Surely the Constitution was more than a mere piece of paper that could be so casually cast aside. Lincoln's conviction in the rightness of the Northern cause helped carry him through the trying years of the war.

Jefferson Davis, the President of the Confederacy, was equally devoted to the Southern cause. He was a firm believer in states' rights and slavery. Even after defeat and two years in prison, he never wavered in his belief that the South was justified in its actions.

Like Lincoln, Jefferson Davis was born in Kentucky. His father, Sam Davis, was a veteran of the Revolutionary War. While Jefferson was still an infant, the Davis family moved to Mississippi. Sam Davis became a successful planter, and young Jeff grew up wealthy and well-educated.

When Davis was sixteen, he received an appointment to the United States Military Academy at West Point, New York. He became an officer and served in the army for seven years. Upon resigning, he married the daughter of his commander, Colonel Zachary Taylor, who later became the twelfth President of the United States.

General Ulysses S. Grant at the time of the siege of Petersburg, Virginia, June 1864.

Davis took his new bride to Mississippi, where he planned to live the life of the gentleman cotton planter. But his wife became ill and died of fever after a three-month illness. Heartbroken and ill himself, Davis traveled for a year to recover from his loss. When he returned to his plantation, he worked hard and became quite wealthy. In 1846 he volunteered and served as a colonel in the Mexican War. His commanding officer again was none other than his former father-in-law, Zachary Taylor, who by that time was a general.

After the Mexican War Davis was elected to the U.S. Senate. Then from 1853 until 1857 he was Secretary of War in the Cabinet of President Franklin Pierce. He followed this service with a second term in the Senate, where he was a fiery spokesman for states' rights. When Abraham Lincoln was elected in 1860 and the Southern states seceded, Davis resigned from the Senate and returned to Mississippi. He had high hopes of becoming the leader of the Confederate Army. He was actually disappointed when he was named President on February 18, 1861.

Jefferson Davis was handsome, well-educated, and experienced in political and military affairs. He had all the qualifications to be a successful leader. Unlike Lincoln, however, he never gained the affection of the people. His government was hindered by jealous officials, independent generals, and a Congress that spent most of its time bickering. Davis's biggest fault was that he tried to manage the government and conduct the war single-handedly. He felt that his way was the only way. He was also hampered by the Confederate Congress's refusal to grant him the power he thought necessary to guide the South successfully through the war.

When Richmond fell to the Union and the war neared its end, Jefferson Davis fled the Confederate capital. He was later captured by Union soldiers and thrown into prison. Charged with being a traitor, he remained imprisoned for two years. He was released in 1867 and lived to the age of eighty-three.

Sadly, a third great Civil War leader did not live to enjoy his later years. Ulysses S. Grant, commander of the Union armies after 1864 and later

From *Everyday Life: The Civil War* ©1999 Good Year Books.

eighteenth President of the United States, died of cancer in 1885 at the age of sixty-three.

Ulysses Simpson Grant was born in Point Pleasant, Ohio, in 1822. He was a shy youth who spent most of his time caring for the animals on his father's farm. He was especially fond of horses. He rode every chance he got and by the time he was twelve was considered an expert horseman. Neighbors were often shocked to see him riding around the countryside standing upright on his saddle.

In 1839 Grant's father got him an appointment to West Point. He proved to be only an average student, but he did excel at horsemanship. Upon becoming a second lieutenant, Grant hoped to be assigned to the cavalry. Unfortunately, there were no openings in the cavalry at the time, and he was placed in the infantry.

Grant fought and served well in the Mexican War of 1846–1848 (although two fellow officers by the names of Jefferson Davis and Robert E. Lee drew more attention). Grant stayed in the army until 1854, when he resigned to return to the civilian world. Attempts at several occupations resulted in failures. At first, Grant tried his hand at farming. When this failed, he worked for a while in a real estate office. Still not satisfied, in 1860 he moved his family to Galena, Illinois, where he worked with his brothers in their father's tannery business. A year later, the Civil War broke out, and Grant once more found himself in the army.

This time he rose quickly in the ranks. Four months after the war's beginning, Grant was a brigadier general. Two years later he was promoted to major general. And in 1864, Lincoln made him a lieutenant general and gave him overall command of the Union armies.

Grant proved to be an able and brilliant commander. His strategy was to find the enemy and strike at him with everything he had. He did not agree with the lightning tactics of such previous commanders as France's Napoleon Bonaparte. Nor did he believe in conducting a limited war, as did Robert E. Lee. Grant's plan of war called for hammering away at the enemy with every means available until his opponent was defeated. In the end this strategy would mean victory for the Union.

Sir Winston Churchill, England's great leader during World War II, paid

General Robert E. Lee, in a picture taken at his home in Richmond shortly after his surrender at Appomattox Court House, Virginia.

From *Everyday Life: The Civil War* ©1999 Good Year Books.

his highest compliment to Grant's opponent on the battlefield: Robert E. Lee. In his writings Churchill recognized Lee as a great leader of men and called him one of the "noblest Americans who ever lived." Quite a compliment for someone who fought on the losing side in a civil war!

Robert E. Lee was born in Virginia in 1807. Both his mother and his father were from well-known Southern families. As a boy, Robert liked to look at paintings of his famous ancestors that hung from the walls of his home in Alexandria. His father, Henry, was perhaps even more famous. He had been one of George Washington's leading generals in the Revolutionary War. Because of his skill as a cavalry officer, Henry Lee was known as "Light-Horse Harry."

Like Jefferson Davis and Ulysses Grant, Lee attained an appointment to West Point. He graduated second in his class in 1829 and went on to a distinguished army career. He was almost ready to retire from service when the Civil War broke out in 1861.

When Virginia left the Union with other Southern states, Lee was faced with a dilemma. He hated slavery and he loved the United States, but he could not bring himself to fight against his home state. After much soul-searching, he resigned from the United States Army and became the commander of the Army of Northern Virginia. Later he was made commander of all the Confederate armies.

Critics of Robert E. Lee are hard to find. He was respected even in the North. His men loved him and would confidently follow him into any battle. He was an expert in strategy and could often figure out what the enemy was planning and strike them before they made their move. One can only wonder how the war might have turned out if Lee had had the same resources at his disposal as Grant.

Few scenes in history were as emotional as Lee's surrender to Grant on April 9, 1865, ending the war. The setting was a house in Appomattox Court House, Virginia. When the terms of surrender were agreed upon, Lee shook hands with Grant and departed the building. He then made one final ride through the ranks of men lining the road outside. As the beloved general passed, Confederate soldiers greeted him with tears streaming down their faces. Many strained to pat Traveller, Lee's famed horse that he rode throughout the war. These ragged survivors knew they had fought for a great leader.

From *Everyday Life: The Civil War* ©1999 Good Year Books.

Name _____ Date _____

Interpret Some Famous Quotes

Here are memorable quotes made by the four leaders mentioned in Chapter 4. On the lines below each, write what you think the quote means.

"A house divided against itself cannot stand."

(Abraham Lincoln speaking before the Republican State Convention in Springfield, Illinois, June 16, 1858)

_____

_____

_____

"Though I have been trained as a soldier and have taken part in many battles, there never has been a time when, in my opinion, some way could not have been found to prevent the drawing of the sword."

(Ulysses Grant, at some point in the Civil War)

_____

_____

_____

"All we ask is to be let alone."

(Jefferson Davis, from his inaugural address, February 18, 1861)

_____

_____

_____

"I believe it to be the duty of every one to unite in the restoration of the country and the re-establishment of peace and harmony."

(Robert E. Lee, after the surrender at Appomattox Court House)

_____

_____

_____

Name _____ Date _____

Name Those Leaders

Write the names of Lincoln, Davis, Grant, or Lee on the blank lines after the statements. Some statements require more than one answer.

1. We were both born in Kentucky. _____ and _____

2. I rode a horse named Traveller. _____

3. I was a failure in every endeavor except the military. _____

4. Each of us graduated from the United States Military Academy at West Point. _____, _____, and _____

5. I was put in prison after the war. _____

6. I refused command of the Union armies when the war began. _____

7. I was born in a log cabin. _____

8. We three fought in the Mexican War. _____, _____, and _____

9. I read books at night by the light of the fireplace. _____

10. As a child, I was an expert horseman. _____

11. I married Zachary Taylor's daughter. _____

12. I walked three miles to return six cents to a lady. _____

13. My father was known as "Light-Horse Harry." _____

14. I could whip most challengers in wrestling and barrel-lifting in my part of Indiana. _____

15. I was the Republican Party's candidate for President in 1860. _____

16. I was disappointed when I was not assigned to the cavalry when I graduated from West Point. _____

17. I have been called a "noble American" by none other than Sir Winston Churchill. _____

From Everyday Life: The Civil War ©1999 Good Year Books.

Name _____ Date _____

Dramatize a Historical Event

Divide the class into groups and have each choose one of the skits. Students should use their imagination and creative skills in planning their skit, which should be about five minutes in length.

Students not participating directly in a skit can make simple props and costumes or critique and rate the skits at the conclusion of the activity.

There is a lead-in to each skit to help students in their planning.

SKIT 1—Lincoln Discussing the Approaching War with His Wife, Mary, and Sons, Todd, Willie, and Tad

As the Southern states seceded and the prospects for peace faded, President Lincoln must have discussed the upcoming war with his family on a number of occasions.

In this skit, portray a likely conversation that took place among family members in their living quarters in the White House.

SKIT 2—Lee's Decision to Resign from the U.S. Army and Cast His Lot with the Confederacy

Lee made a most difficult decision when he turned down President Lincoln's offer to command the Union forces and instead resigned his commission.

This skit should be centered around the reasons for his decision. A dialogue could be planned reflecting a conversation that might have taken place between Lee and his wife, Mary, and other officers and their wives at a social gathering.

SKIT 3—The Signing of the Terms of Surrender at Appomattox Court House

Grant was most gracious to Lee when the terms of surrender were discussed. Confederate soldiers were not treated as prisoners of war but were permitted to return immediately to their homes. They also were allowed to keep their horses to work their farms.

Center this skit on the conversation that took place around the conference table.

SKIT 4—Reaction to Jefferson Davis's Imprisonment As a Traitor

There was strong reaction in both the North and the South to the imprisonment of Jefferson Davis after the war.

Plan this skit to reflect either view: that of a group in the North lauding the action, or that of a group in the South condemning it.

CHAPTER 5

The Soldier's Life

The men and boys on both sides who marched off to fight the Civil War quickly learned the hard facts of army life. Only about 10 percent of their time was actually devoted to fighting; the other 90 percent was taken up by drilling and marching. In the field they learned to sleep in damp tents and survive on the barest of rations. They found ways to cope with homesickness and boredom. They reluctantly came to accept stern discipline and the loss of individual freedom. Almost overnight, the glamour of being a soldier was tarnished by the realities of camp life.

Very little training took place in the early months of the war. Both sides hurried to rush troops into battle before the other was ready. Many soldiers had only two or three weeks of training, some even less. A number of youthful recruits and drummer boys went directly from their schoolrooms to the battlefield. In reality neither the North or the South believed that their differences would actually break out into a war. They trusted in yet another compromise to keep the peace. Thus, when the guns started firing, nobody was prepared for all-out war.

Two soldiers pose for a studio portrait. Such pictures were popular at the beginning of the war, when everyone thought the fighting would not last long.

Early training left much to be desired. Recruits grumbled about the constant drilling, although they finally came to realize such was necessary to move and position soldiers in battle. On both sides weapons were at first limited to old muskets dating from Revolutionary War days. Many soldiers had no weapons at all and had to drill with wooden guns and swords. Some even had to resort to using cornstalks!

When it came to drilling troops, the Confederate Army had a decided advantage. The bulk of the experienced officers and soldiers in the United State Army had resigned and joined the Confederacy. Also, seven of the eight military schools in the nation were located in the South. Therefore the South had officers who knew how to train men. The success of Confederate troops early in the war can be attributed to their being better trained and disciplined to maintain their composure under fire.

Many soldiers not only trained with outdated muskets, but fought with them early in the war. This was especially true on the Confederate side. A

From *Everyday Life: The Civil War* ©1999 Good Year Books.

musket fired a round ball that had to be rammed, along with powder, down the muzzle. Since this required a number of movements on the part of the soldier, no more than two or three shots could be gotten off in a minute.

As the fighting progressed, rifles that fired cone-shaped bullets came into use. These weapons were much more deadly than the earlier muskets. Then, halfway through the war, the repeating rifle appeared. It enabled a soldier to fire from five to seven shots without reloading. The repeating rifle was partly responsible for the enormous number of casualties on both sides.

Because no one expected the war to last long, soldiers marched off to fight in a wide variety of uniforms. Many were homemade. Both Billy Yank and Johnny Reb sported a rainbow of colors. Some units wore baggy red trousers, purple blouses, and red fezzes. (A fez is a red, cone-shaped hat with a flat top and tassel, native to the Turks.) One Northern regiment departed for fame and glory dressed in kilts!

Pictures of the time show many soldiers at first simply dressed in their own clothes. When a regiment of troopers did have uniforms, likely as not the colors would be blue if they were Rebels and gray if they were Yanks. This resulted in much confusion and a few mishaps on the battlefield. When standardized uniforms were finally adopted, they often misfitted and made the wearer look a little foolish. In time, most Union troops wore blue and their Confederate opponents wore butternut, a light brownish gray. This led to Union soldiers being called "Bluebellies" and Confederate troopers "Butternuts." Many Butternuts rounded out their attire with straw hats.

No soldier's uniform included a set of dog tags. Dog tags, metal identification disks worn around the neck, did not come into use until wars later. The absence of any kind of identification tag explains the tremendous number of graves with headstones marked "Unknown Soldier." As the war wore on and casualties increased, men on both sides began to sew their names on their uniforms previous to a battle. Others just simply wrote their names on a piece of paper and pinned it to their blouses.

If an army "marches on its stomach," as Napoleon Bonaparte once said, then Civil War armies marched on stomachs that were often empty. Soldiers, at least in theory, were supposed to have eggs, milk, butter, wheat flour, and sugar to go along with their usual fare of hardtack, salt pork, dried beef, beans, and potatoes. In reality, provisions of any kind were often scarce and hard to come by.

In 1864 the Union soldier each day was supposed to get 20 ounces of beef, 18 ounces of flour, 2.56 ounces of dry beans, 1.6 ounces of coffee, 2.4 ounces of sugar, and lesser amounts of such things as salt, pepper, and vinegar (as well as soap). Complain as he might, the Union soldier lived like a king compared to his Confederate counterpart. One-hundred Confederate soldiers were expected to get by on ¼ pound of bacon, 18 ounces of flour, and 10 pounds of rice over a thirty-day period.

Although both armies condemned it, soldiers often resorted to foraging to satisfy their hunger. To forage means to live off the land. In its simplest form, foraging consisted of hunting and gathering nuts and berries. But all too often both sides took foods and livestock from nearby farmers, sometimes at gunpoint.

Soldiers who had enough money could supplement their drab diet by buying foodstuffs (and other items) from sutlers. Sutlers were peddlers who followed the armies with wagonloads of goods. Often they bought stolen merchandise and sold it at several times the purchase price. To get a dozen eggs, a soldier might have to pay a sutler as much as six dollars. A pound of bacon often sold for fifteen dollars!

A refreshment and embarkation center in Philadelphia, where enlistees paused on their way to war. From an old lithograph.

Considering such prices and the monthly pay of the average soldier, a sutler's goods often went unsold. At the beginning of the war, both sides paid privates $11 a month. Eventually a Union private received $16 and a Confederate private $18. Not exactly the kind of pay with which to enrich the sutler!

Low pay and inadequate food were not the only complaints of the Civil War soldier. Shelter left something to be desired as well. While fighting was taking place, troops on both sides slept on the ground in tents that accommodated from four to twelve persons. Such closeness created a major problem when, in the middle of the night, one of the sleepers decided to change position. Usually the men agreed that when one of them wanted to turn over he would awaken the others. Then, on a prearranged signal, they all would turn in the same direction at once.

From *Everyday Life: The Civil War* ©1999 Good Year Books.

Since little fighting was done during the winter, soldiers might stay in one place for several months. This enabled them to create more permanent quarters. Sometimes they were able to build sturdy log cabins with real roofs and chimneys. More often, however, their shelters consisted of cabins with log walls and tent roofs. The walls might be from twelve to twenty feet long and five feet high. At each end a forked stick supported a crosspiece over which was stretched a number of canvas tents buttoned together. If the tent roof consisted of two thicknesses of canvas, it was usually strong enough to keep out rain and snow.

A Union drummer boy. Some drummer boys were as young as nine. Many drummers were killed in battle.

Soldiers completed their makeshift cabins with chimneys of sticks or barrels. Often these caught on fire, much to the amusement of any civilians who happened to be passing by. Inside, soldiers sometimes decorated the log walls of the cabin with pictures of ladies cut from popular magazines of the day. Even to the Civil War soldier, "pin-ups" helped ease the pang of homesickness.

Boredom was another problem for soldiers. While in camp, many passed the time playing such games as checkers and horseshoes. Others wrote letters or gathered to sing songs. Raffles were also popular, be they for a fresh five-dollar bill or a fresh live chicken. Horse races and foot races took up many hours, and when these became humdrum, soldiers thought of different kinds of contests. In one camp it was reported that a group of soldiers drew a racetrack on a piece of canvas and bet and screamed for their favorite louse as it scurried along the course. With lice a huge health problem in most camps, louse races may have been common.

If homesickness sometimes struck the older troops, it was especially hard on the younger soldiers and the boys who had signed on as drummers. Some drummer boys were as young as nine. Can you picture yourself going into battle at the age of nine? (One nine-year-old drummer boy named Johnny Clem picked up a rifle and actually fought alongside his fellow soldiers. Although wounded, he finished the war as a thirteen-year-old sergeant! Some estimates claim that as many as 10 to 20 percent of the soldiers in the Civil War were under the age of sixteen!)

The discomforts of army life were small problems compared to diseases that raged through the camps. Of the 620,000 soldiers who perished in the war, over 400,000 died of sickness and disease. Smallpox, pneumonia, measles, and dysentery were the ever present companions of the Civil War soldier.

Name _____ Date _____

Create a Camp Dialogue

The Civil War was the last war in which drummer boys saw service. At least 40,000 boys served as drummers in the Union Army and 20,000 in the Confederate. Some were as young as nine. Many of these boys were killed.

Drums were an important means of communication on the battlefield. The *thrump, thrump, thrump* of the drums helped troops locate their units amid the noise and smoke surrounding them, and told soldiers how to position themselves.

Drummer boys, like other soldiers, feared going into battle. Create a dialogue between two drummer boys that might have occurred on the eve of their introduction to war.

Name _____ Date _____

Bake a Batch of Corn Dodgers

Soldiers in the field, if they happened to have the proper ingredients, sometimes would make corn dodgers. A corn dodger is a stiff or hard bread made of fried or baked corn meal. Plain as they may sound, corn dodgers provided a little variety to the usual diet of hardtack and beans.

Some corn-dodger recipes today call for eggs as one of the ingredients. But since Civil War soldiers rarely had access to eggs, they probably made their corn dodgers using a recipe similar to this one.

You can make a batch of corn dodgers yourself in a matter of minutes. Ask your parents or another adult to help you.

Corn Dodgers

1 cup corn meal   2 tablespoons melted butter or margarine

1 teaspoon salt   Cold water

1 aluminum baking pan

a piece of greased aluminum foil (optional)

Steps:

1. Mix the corn meal with the salt and butter.

2. Add just enough water to the dough so you can make it into little rolls with your hands.

3. Place the rolls in a greased pan and bake for 30 minutes at 325° F. (Since ovens vary, you many have to turn the oven down to 300° F.)

Your parents or the adult helping you will think you're extremely clever if you suggest that the inside of the baking pan be lined with a piece of greased aluminum foil before the rolls are put in. That way, there will be no mess to clean up after the corn dodgers are ready.

Name _____ Date _____

Put On Your Thinking Cap

Put on your thinking cap and write your best answers to these questions. Continue your answers on a separate sheet of paper. A score of 100 percent indicates that your thinking cap is critically adjusted.

1. A large number of soldiers in both the Union and the Confederate armies were under the age of sixteen. Some were as young as thirteen. These boys were not drummer boys but actual fighting soldiers. What do you think might account for so many of them being able to openly enlist despite their ages?

_____

_____

_____

_____

_____

2. Fraternization, or associating with others in a friendly way, occurred quite often among people on opposite sides of the Civil War. This was especially true regarding pickets. Pickets were soldiers sent ahead of the main army to check on what the enemy was doing. On many occasions pickets of the opposing armies, instead of firing on each other, met and exchanged pleasantries. They often sat and talked of home and traded food and tobacco. Why do you think fraternization between enemy forces occurred more frequently during the Civil War than in other wars involving Americans?

_____

_____

_____

3. You have learned that more than 600,000 soldiers died in the Civil War. Some estimates even place the number as high as 700,000. New weapons, along with disease and sickness, accounted for the majority of these casualties. But can you think of an outdated military tactic that also resulted in the unnecessary deaths of thousands more?

_____

_____

_____

_____

From *Everyday Life: The Civil War* ©1999 Good Year Books.

Name _____ Date _____

Interpret a Pie Graph

The Civil War has often been referred to by historians as a "boys' war." In the Union Army alone, 80% of the men in arms were under the age of twenty-three. The percentage may have been even higher in the Confederate Army, where a shortage of manpower was always a problem.

The graph below shows by percentage the age groups of the soldiers who fought for the Union.

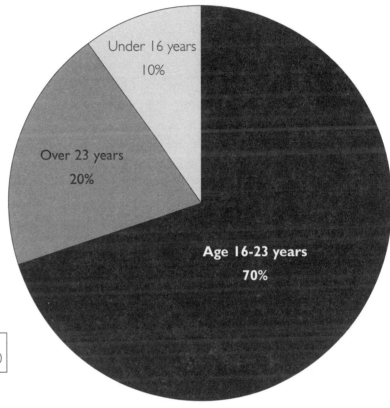

Age of Union Soldiers

Under 16 years
10%

Over 23 years
20%

Age 16-23 years
70%

Total Number of Soldiers: 2,500,000

Use the graph to answer the questions below.

1. How many Union soldiers were under the age of 16?
    _____

2. How many soldiers were between the ages of 16 and 23?
    _____

3. How many were over 23 years of age?
    _____

CHAPTER 6

The Home Fronts

While soldiers in wartime face each other at the front, or battle zone, civilians back home are involved in another kind of front. Their front is called the "home front." Young and old alike do all they can to help in the war effort by collecting food and other supplies to be sent to the soldiers in the field. Often they make great sacrifices and suffer tremendous deprivations in the process.

Civilian hardships at home were greater in the Civil War than in any other war in American history. Many families had little to eat, especially in the South, where a large number of people actually died from starvation. Other families got by on the barest of provisions.

But shortages and hardships were not problems in the early months of the war. No one expected the fighting to last long, and most people at home in both the North and the South pitched in to help. Women made uniforms, knitted clothes, and rolled bandages. They worked in plants making shells and cartridges. Many served in hospitals caring for the sick and wounded.

Women on both sides contributed much to the war effort. This picture from the July 20, 1861, issue of *Harper's Weekly* magazine features a group of women making cartridges in a munitions plant in Maine.

Children also did their part. Girls sewed towels and knitted socks, while boys helped the wives of men who had gone off to war by chopping firewood and tending to crops and livestock. Because shortages appeared early in the South, children there were called on to make special sacrifices. They ate less to conserve food and went barefoot in warm weather to save leather.

The way families lived in the North depended on their economic status. Some factory owners tripled their profits in making supplies for the army and consequently lived quite well. The same was true of farmers who greatly increased their wheat production to feed the troops.

But for the average Northern family, life was difficult during the war years. Most workers labored from ten to twelve hours a day and often earned less than $3.00. At that wage one could barely feed his or her family. Prices rose more than 50 percent, and even topped 75 percent later in the war. Foods such as eggs and bacon became so expensive that the average consumer

From *Everyday Life: The Civil War* ©1999 Good Year Books.

could not buy them. As a result, Northerners got by on a diet consisting chiefly of meat and potatoes.

Confederate money became almost worthless as the war wore on. This one-hundred dollar note bought little in the South in 1865.

As the war wore on, people in the South would have been thrilled to have had meat and potatoes. Often, any food at all was hard to come by. Children searched the countryside for nuts and berries, and many people were reduced to eating rats. Several factors accounted for such deplorable conditions. At the onset of the war, the North blockaded Southern ports, making it extremely difficult for any kind of supplies to come in. The situation became even more severe when Union troops called bummers raided farms and took produce and livestock. Sometimes soldiers maliciously destroyed precious foodstuffs, pouring honey and molasses over the furniture in houses they had ransacked. Finally, trains that might have otherwise brought in and distributed food broke down from lack of Northern parts.

Confederate money eventually became worthless and prices soared. Near the end of the war, a pound of butter cost $15 and a barrel of flour, $1,000! Coffee rose to an astronomical $70 a pound. If someone wanted to purchase a chicken, he or she had to come up with $50. A pair of fish cost the same. Even turnip greens sold for $4 a peck. Think of such prices in light of a Confederate soldier earning only $16 a month!

The price of other goods also skyrocketed. A pair of boots might cost $250 and a good coat $100 more. Not even simple household items escaped such huge increases. Mary Boykin Chesnut, an aristocratic lady from Charleston, South Carolina, wrote in 1865 that she paid $50 for a small wooden bucket. The same bucket would have cost $0.25 before the war!

To make up for the high price of some goods and the scarcity of others, Southern women displayed a lot of ingenuity. They made clothing out of rags and curtains and fashioned shoes from such materials as old carpets and canvas sails. Since needles were hard to find, they made pins out of neatly cut thorns. For buttons they used dried persimmon seeds. To add color to cloth, they used onion skins to obtain a burnt-orange dye and carrot tops to make a dye of greenish yellow.

Southerners improvised in the same way regarding food. Tea was brewed from dried berry leaves and coffee from wheat, corn, toasted yams, or okra seeds. Baking soda was made from the ashes of corncobs, and molasses and

Buildings in New York City burn in July 1863, as rioters protest a draft law passed by Congress. In three days of violence, hundreds are killed or injured and property losses totaled $1,500,000.

honey took the place of sugar. Salt was obtained by several methods. One was to boil saltwater until the water evaporated. Another was to dig up the dirt under smokehouses, where salt had fallen off meat that had previously been dried.

The food situation was so desperate in the South by 1863 that food riots broke out in a number of cities. One of the first riots occurred in the Confederate capital of Richmond. A lady named Mary Jackson led three hundred women into the city on April 2, demanding food. The women insisted that they be allowed to buy food at the same prices the army paid. When their request was ignored, they were joined by a number of bystanders, and the combined group became a mob that broke into a number of stores. They carried off groceries, baked goods, and shoes. Jefferson Davis himself arrived by carriage and pleaded with the women to go home. In the end, he had to threaten to have troops fire on them before they consented to leave.

The North was plagued by riots of a different nature. There the complaint centered around the draft. At first, men heeded President Lincoln's call for volunteers and rushed to enlist in droves. But as the war wore on, the number of volunteers dwindled. In 1863 Congress passed a draft law that met with stiff opposition. Northerners resented the fact that the law allowed a person with three hundred dollars to pay a substitute to go to war in his place. This made it possible for men with money to stay home while the poor and not-so-fortunate had to march off to fight.

From *Everyday Life: The Civil War* ©1999 Good Year Books.

The worst draft riot occurred in New York City in July 1863. It lasted for three days and resulted in more than 2,000 casualties. Mobs burned the local draft office and a number of buildings and homes. Federal troops had to be called in to put an end to the disturbance.

Near the end of the war, as city after city in the South fell into Union hands, a new problem arose. That was the problem of refugees. Both blacks and whites took to the roads: slaves who had been freed or had run away, and Southerners fleeing the advance of the Union Army. Narrow dirt roads were often clogged with hundreds of thousands of people on the move.

Some sources estimate that as many as half of a million ex-slaves followed the Union Army as it swept through the South. A large number served the troops as nurses, cooks, laundresses, and laborers. Tens of thousands of black males were accepted into the army, where they fought valiantly. Their story will be told in a later chapter.

As many as 250,000 white Southerners became refugees also. A large number of these were women and children. Many fled to the countryside, carrying their belongings in carts and wagons. Others set out for cities and towns less likely to come under attack. Regardless of where they went, fear and hunger followed them.

The shortage of food and supplies was compounded with Union General William T. Sherman's "march to the sea" in the last months of the war. Beginning in November 1864, Union troops burned and destroyed everything in their path from Atlanta to Savannah, Georgia. They purposely ruined crops and anything else that would break the Southern will to fight. For three hundred miles, little was left within a stretch some sixty miles wide. Even railroad tracks were pulled up, heated over fires, and wrapped around trees like pretzels.

After reaching Savannah, the Union army continued into South Carolina, where they burned the city of Columbia to the ground. The march did not end until the army swept through North Carolina to the sea. The trail of destruction caused bitterness and hatred that lingered in the South for many years after the war had ended.

Union soldiers fashion "Sherman pretzels" as they wrap heated rails around trees during Sherman's march to the sea in December 1864. Such destruction added to the bitterness that lingered in the South long after the war ended.

Name _____ Date _____

Finish a Story

Slaves sometimes were faced with a difficult decision as Union soldiers approached the plantations on which they labored. Should they stay and help the master's family as best they could, or should they run away and follow the Union troops to freedom?

At right is a story that has been started for you. On the lines provided, complete the story, giving it any ending you choose. Continue on a sheet of notebook paper, if necessary.

Thomas Parker, his wife Julia, and their two children sat excitedly in their small cabin discussing the approach of the Union Army. Each offered his or her opinion as to what they should do.

"I just don't think it's right to leave Miss Constance and her daughters to fend for themselves," said Thomas. "Why, those women have never had to lift a finger at anything. They'd starve to death in a minute!"

"How can you feel for them?" asked Julia. "Before Master James left, he told Miss Constance to flail the daylights out of us if we disobeyed her. I say we leave and we leave now. The Union soldiers will take care of us."

"Yes, Papa," exclaimed Jenny, his young daughter. "Let's go! We aren't beholden to Miss Constance at all. I don't care what happens to her and her prissy daughters!"

As Jenny's brother Charles nodded in agreement, the first Union troops could be seen approaching the plantation from the west, no more than a few hundred yards away.

Name _____ Date _____

Were These Incidents Justified?

In Chapter 6 you read about food riots in the South and draft riots in the North. You also read about the high prices people (especially in the South) paid for food and other needed products. Finally, you learned of Sherman's ruinous "march to the sea" near the end of the war.

On the lines provided, explain whether you think each or any of these incidents were justified. Give reasons for your answers.

1. Southern food riots

_____
_____
_____

2. Draft riots in the North

_____
_____
_____

3. High prices

_____
_____
_____

4. Sherman's "march to the sea"

_____
_____
_____

Name _____ Date _____

Fill In a Venn Diagram

Fill in the Venn diagram below to compare life in the North and the South during the Civil War. Write facts about each in the appropriate place. List characteristics common to both where the circles overlap.

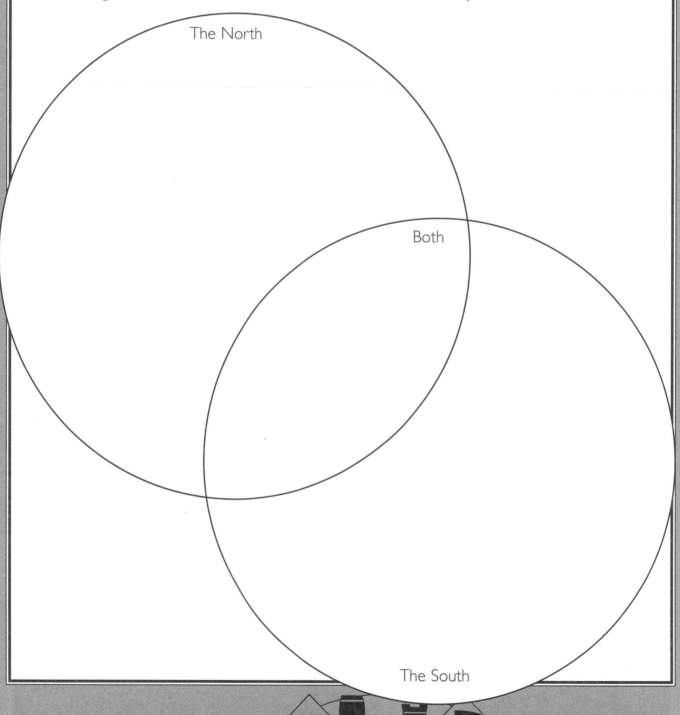

The North

Both

The South

Name _____ Date _____

Solve Some Home-Front Word Problems

Use the spaces provided to answer the word problems.

1. A lady in the North worked 12 hours a day, 6 days a week, in a textile mill. She earned a total of $3.00 for each day's work.

   a. What was her hourly wage?
      $_____

   b. If 95% of her weekly earnings were spent feeding her family, how much did she spend each week for food?
      $_____

   c. How much money did she have left to purchase other items?
      $_____

2. Look back through Chapter 6 and find the cost of a pound of coffee in the South near the end of the war. Then find the monthly pay of a Confederate soldier at that same time.

   a. How many months would a soldier have had to save his entire pay to buy a pound of coffee? (Show a decimal and round to the nearest tenth.)
      _____ months

   b. How many month's pay was necessary to purchase a pair of pants that cost $100? (Show a fraction.)
      _____ months

3. Assume that the average cost of a pair of shoes in the North in 1861 was $15. If the price of the shoes increased by 50% in four years, how much did they cost by the end of the war?
      $_____

From *Everyday Life: The Civil War* ©1999 Good Year Books.

CHAPTER 7

Innovations

The Civil War started out much like the wars before it: formations of troops lined up in neat rows and advanced toward the enemy, firing outdated, muzzle-loading muskets. The enemy, in turn, fired back with their outdated, muzzle-loading muskets. Nobody considered hiding behind trees or digging trenches for concealment. To do so would have been thought cowardly and not consistent with the accepted rules of warfare.

You learned in a previous chapter that the age-old tactic of troops advancing in row after row continued until the latter part of the war. What finally caused this strategy to be changed was the unbelievable slaughter manifested by the introduction of deadly new weapons. Cannons that fired 300-pound cannonballs appeared. These same cannons could also hurl nails and chains into the midst of neatly packed rows of advancing soldiers. Cone-shaped bullets and repeating rifles further added to the slaughter, as did improved mortars and other artillery pieces. Even an early kind of machine gun saw limited used.

Soldiers stand next to a Whitworth cannon, a typical artillery piece used in the Civil War.

But new guns alone did not make the Civil War different from previous wars. Many other innovations appeared. The wide use of railroads and the telegraph made the conflict the first "modern war." So did the use of ironclad ships and observation balloons.

A few changes that occurred were relatively simple. Some historians say that Robert E. Lee's greatest innovation in warfare was the spade, or shovel. When it became apparent that the South could not match the North's firepower, Lee had his troops start digging trenches and smaller holes for one or two soldiers, nowadays known as foxholes. The North also eventually adopted the same methods.

Not all innovations had to do with weapons and tactics. For the first time, large numbers of newspaper and magazine reporters covered the war's events. So did photographers. Your history text may contain pictures taken by Matthew Brady. Brady followed the armies throughout the war, making photographs of soldiers, camp life, and battle scenes. Also, his pictures of Abraham Lincoln are among the best on record.

From *Everyday Life: The Civil War* ©1999 Good Year Books.

Some changes that occurred during the war affected civilians. Not all such changes were met with enthusiasm. You read about draft riots in the last chapter. Another change had to do with taxes. To help finance the war, the U.S. Congress passed the first income-tax law on August 5, 1861. Taxes were also levied for the first time on tobacco and cigarettes.

Soldiers of the railroad construction corps could construct such a bridge in a matter of days. From a Mathew Brady photograph.

But the majority of innovations during the Civil War years were connected with the military. One of the most important concerned railroads. Here, the North held a decided advantage. Some 72 percent of the railroad tracks in the United States lay within Union territory. This percent increased greatly as Union forces captured rail lines in Virginia, Tennessee, Alabama, and Mississippi. Control of the railroads enabled the North to rush men, supplies, and ammunition almost anywhere that fighting was taking place.

Although its track mileage was limited, the South benefited nonetheless from the rail system. At the First Battle of Bull Run, in July 1861, General Irvin McDowell's Union troops were about to achieve victory when Confederate General Joseph Johnston came to the rescue with 10,000 men aboard the Manassas Gap Railroad. The arrival of these additional soldiers helped turn the tide of battle in favor of the Confederacy.

The introduction of balloons to warfare coincided with several other firsts. Boats were converted into "aircraft carriers" capable of launching observation balloons from their decks. And in June 1861 a man named Thaddeus Lowe sent the first telegraphic message from the air. The message was sent to President Lincoln over a line that extended from Lowe's balloon to a receiver on the ground at the White House.

The Union's first attempt to use an observation balloon in combat ended in disaster. As the device was being rushed by wagon to Bull Run in 1861, it was ripped apart by treetops before reaching its destination. At best, the Union never

An early Union observation balloon. Both sides used balloons to check on the enemy.

had more than six balloons that were operational at one time. Balloonists checked on enemy positions and communicated with their own forces on the ground by dropping messages over the side.

The presence of a Union balloon in the sky one night early in the fighting brought about another military innovation: the first blackout in wartime. Confederate General P. G. T. Beauregard ordered all camp lights covered and dimmed to thwart the balloonists' attempt to determine the strength of his army by counting the number of tent lights.

The Monitor and the Merrimac fire at each other off the coast of Virginia, March 9, 1862. The three-hour battle ended in a draw.

The South had few balloons, and bad luck deprived them of even those. An incident that occurred in the summer of 1862 illustrates the point well. Someone suggested that the ladies of the Confederacy donate their silk dresses to be used as fabric in the construction of an observation balloon. The call went out, and the ladies responded with patriotic fervor. A balloon was made and shipped by railroad and steamer toward the site of an important battle. But before the steamer completed its journey down the James River, the tide went out and the boat got stuck on a sandbar. Much to the dismay of the Confederacy, the balloon fell into Union hands. In one stroke of misfortune, the South lost its prized airship and a good number of its silk dresses.

Another innovation of the war was the first use of ironclad ships. Shortly after the fighting began, the South converted a sunken Union steamer named the *Merrimac* into an armor-plated vessel that they called the *Virginia*. The Union in turn built an ironclad warship they called the *Monitor*. The two craft met and slugged it out for four hours off the Virginia coast on March 9, 1862. Thousands of spectators watched and cheered from the shore as cannonball after cannonball bounced off the hulls of both ships, causing only minor dents. Not a single sailor on either side was hurt. The fight ended in a draw.

Neither the *Virginia* nor the *Monitor* saw much action afterwards. In May 1862 the Confederacy scuttled (purposely sank) the *Virginia* to keep it from falling into Union hands. And on December 31, 1862, the *Monitor* sank in a

From *Everyday Life: The Civil War* ©1999 Good Year Books.

gale off the coast of Cape Hatteras, North Carolina. The appearance of the *Virginia* and the *Monitor* brought a close to the age of the wooden warship. Henceforth, all ships of war would be constructed of iron.

The use of railroads, balloons, and ironclad ships—along with improved rifles and cannons—were but a few of the new developments introduced during the Civil War. There were many others. Railway guns, land mines, and hand grenades appeared for the first time. So did flame-throwers, telescopic sights for rifles, and revolving gun turrets. And after troops on both sides starting digging in for safety, wire entanglements and periscopes for trenches were introduced.

Along with the more practical devices put into use came a number of wacky inventions. One was a cannon with a forked barrel that shot two chained-together cannon balls at the same time. Its inventor boasted that the device would mow down row after row of enemy soldiers. Whether enemy soldiers would have consented to stay in one place and be mowed down by the chained cannon balls will never be known, for the weapon never found its way onto the battlefield.

Another invention was supposed to eliminate the need for military bridges. It consisted of soldiers wearing miniature canoes on their feet and propelling themselves across the water with paddles! Like the forked-barrel cannon, the canoe shoes never found a buyer.

A final innovation of the Civil War was concerned with saving lives, rather than destroying them: the first organized medical and nursing corps for wartime. A private organization called the United States Sanitary Commission eased the suffering of the wounded on both sides. It operated private hospitals and delivered needed supplies. Its work was of great benefit to the medical departments of both the Union and Confederate governments.

Some three thousand women served as nurses, an occupation which until the war had been reserved almost exclusively for men. Many, like Clara Barton, who later founded the American Red Cross, worked in field hospitals directly on the battlefield. Both the stories of hospitals and the heroic women who staffed them will be covered in later chapters.

Workers at a U.S. Sanitary Commission site. The Sanitary Commission was formed to care for the wounded and to improve hygiene in the camps.

Name _____ Date _____

Solve an Innovations Puzzle

Fill in the sentences for clues to complete the puzzle about new developments that took place during the Civil War.

```
    _ I _ _
    _ _ N _ _ _ _ _
_ _ _ _ _ _ N
    _ O _ _
    V _ _ _ _ _ _ _ _
    _ _ A _ _
_ _ _ _ T
    _ _ _ I _ _ _ _
_ _ _ _ O _ _ _
    _ _ N _ _ _ _ _
    _ _ S _ _ _ _
```

1. The Confederacy once made an observation balloon from _____ dresses.

2. The _____ fought the *Virginia* to a draw in March 1862.

3. Clara _____ founded the American Red Cross.

4. Thaddeus _____ sent the first telegraphic message from a balloon.

5. After the *Merrimac* was raised and converted to an ironclad ship, its name was changed to the _____.

6. Matthew _____ was a famous Civil War photographer.

7. A violent _____ riot occurred in New York City in opposition to the war.

8. The United States _____ Commission helped the wounded of both the North and the South.

9. _____ were used for aerial observation for the first time during the Civil War.

10. Some Southern troops arrived at the First Battle of Bull Run by way of the _____ Gap Railroad.

11. The muzzle-loading _____ was used by most soldiers at the beginning of the Civil War.

From *Everyday Life: The Civil War* ©1999 Good Year Books.

Name _____ Date _____

Use Context Clues to Complete Sentences

Here is a brief account of the first balloon flights in history. Fill in the blanks in the sentences of the story using the words below.

along

crashing

descending

distance

event

flew

height

heroes

landed

later

launched

passengers

place

rewarded

safely

some time

town

used

Although balloons were _____ in the Civil War, they were not new inventions. People had been ascending (and often _____ very quickly) in the air-filled devices for _____.

The very first balloon was _____ in June 1783. The site of the historic _____ was the small French _____ of Annonay. There the brothers Jacques and Joseph Montgolfier sent their balloon to a _____ of 6,000 feet.

Three months _____, the Montgolfiers launched their balloon again. This time it carried three _____: a sheep, a duck, and a rooster. The balloon flew for eight minutes and landed _____. All three of the animals emerged with something of a reputation as local _____. The sheep, in fact, was _____ with a permanent _____ in the royal zoo of King Louis XVI.

In November 1783 the first humans went aloft in the Montgolfiers' balloon. They _____ for about 25 minutes and covered a _____ of 5 miles. They _____ safely despite almost _____ into rooftops and windmills _____ the way.

Name _____ Date _____

Improve Your Map Skills

ook in an atlas, encyclopedia, or other source containing maps and fill in the blanks in the paragraphs.

1. The *Monitor* and the *Merrimac (Virginia)* battled off the coast at Hampton Roads, Virginia, on March 9, 1862. Hampton Roads is not a road or city. It is a _____.
   Three rivers meet in Virginia at Hampton Roads. They are the _____, the _____, and the _____. To reach Hampton Roads from _____, Virginia's capital, one would travel _____ (in which direction?).

2. Two states border Virginia on the south. They are _____ and _____. The capitals of these states are _____ and _____.
   Virginia is bordered on the west by the states of _____ and _____. The capitals of these states are _____ and _____.

3. To the northeast, Virginia borders the city of _____, which makes up the entire District of _____. The city is located on the _____ River. This river forms the northeast boundary between Virginia and the state of _____.

4. If you were to fly in a straight line from Richmond, Virginia, to Charleston, West Virginia, you would cross two ranges of the Appalachian Mountains. They are the _____ Mountains and the _____ Mountains.

Name _____ Date _____

Draw a Cartoon

Draw a cartoon illustrating what you think a Civil War soldier might have looked like paddling across a river wearing tiny canoes on his feet. Give your cartoon a clever caption.

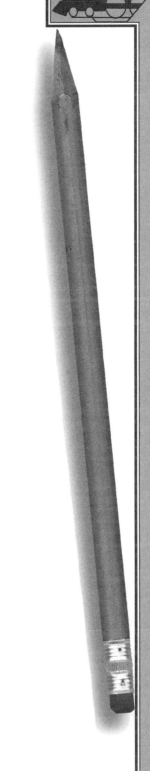

Unusual and Interesting Facts

Like all wars, the Civil War has its share of interesting and unusual facts and occurrences. Space limitations make it possible to tell only a few of these.

Perhaps the most unusual aspect of the Civil War was the youth of the soldiers involved. In Chapter 5 you learned that approximately 250,000 of the participating troops were under the age of sixteen. This means that as many as 10 percent were no more than children. And this number is a conservative estimate.

The need for drummer and bugle boys accounts for the youngest of the enlistees. Boys seeking adventure or bored with life on the farm signed up in droves. But boys a few years older managed to slip past recruiters and fight as regular soldiers. In an age before driver's licenses and social security numbers, recruiters had no way of checking the age of an enlistee. It was relatively easy for a tall, husky farm boy of twelve to pass for seventeen or eighteen.

The South seemed to be more lax than the North in allowing young boys to enlist. Probably this was because of the shortage of manpower in the Confederate Army. A quick look at some boys and their ages will show how desperate the South must have been for recruits.

George S. Lampkin of Mississippi enlisted at the age of eleven and was severely wounded at Shiloh when he was twelve. Kentuckian E. G. Baxter joined up at the age of thirteen and one year later was a second lieutenant. John Tyler of Maryland enlisted when he was twelve and fought the entire war without receiving a single wound. M. W. Jewett of Virginia joined the 59th Virginia Regiment when only thirteen. A host of other boys were fourteen and up. And these youngsters were infantrymen, not drummers or buglers!

Even the officers in the war were young. Brevet Major General Galusha Pennypacker of the Union Army was at seventeen the youngest general. The youngest Confederate general was William Paul Roberts, who was twenty. And you are probably familiar with General George Armstrong Custer, who eleven years after the Civil War was killed by the Sioux Indians at the Battle of the Little Bighorn in southern Montana. Custer became a brigadier general of cavalry during the Civil War at the age of twenty-three.

An extremely young soldier, perhaps a military school cadet, poses in formal uniform, complete with a rifle almost as long as he is high.

From *Everyday Life: The Civil War* ©1999 Good Year Books.

Youth was never more apparent than at the Battle of New Market, Virginia, on May 15, 1864. The battle was rather insignificant except for the ages of some of the participants. A group of 247 cadets from the Virginia Military Institute at Lexington marched to New Market to join a Confederate force of 4,500. All of the cadets were eighteen and under. Some were thought to be as young as fourteen. Their commander, Professor and Lieutenant Colonel Scott Shipp, was the "old man" of the group at 24. The boys from VMI were instrumental in helping take a hill from which Federal cannon pounded away at the Confederates. With fixed bayonets, the cadets charged wildly ahead and helped rout the Union battery (one unit of the Army). Ten of the cadets were killed and forty-seven were wounded.

A young soldier poses for the camera before marching off to war.

The young ages of many soldiers was but one unusual aspect of the Civil War. Another was the use of tens of thousands of foreigners to fight for both sides. Foreign troops represented almost every nationality and ethnic group. From western Europe there were Germans, Irish, French, Scotch, Spaniards, Swiss, Dutch, Scandinavians, and Englishmen. From southern and eastern Europe came Italians, Poles, Hungarians, and Russian Cossacks. And from the northern and southern sections of North America came a large number of Canadians and Mexicans to join in the conflict.

A number of the foreign soldiers were veterans of European wars. One grizzled old veteran, who died at the battle of Shiloh in Tennessee, had fought against Napoleon Bonaparte at Waterloo in 1815! He was over 70 years of age when he was killed. Others had served in various wars, including the Crimean War of 1854–1856.

A number of foreigners held titles of nobility. There were more than fifty titled German officers in the Union Army alone. Two French royal princes, Louis Philippe Albert d'Orleans and Eugene Ferdinand d'Orleans, served on the staff of Union General George McClellan. Each traveled about with his own company of servants.

Most foreigners, however, were common foot soldiers. Often entire companies and regiments were composed of men of one nationality. In such cases, language was never a serious problem. But consider the case of the

From Everyday Life: The Civil War ©1999 Good Year Books.

1st Louisiana Regiment of the Confederate Army. It contained men of thirty-seven different nationalities!

Some foreign soldiers went through the entire war understanding little that was said to them. One in particular was a German who fought with the Army of Northern Virginia. Seldom comprehending what was going on around him, he always camped apart in a crude hut made of leaves and branches. Fellow soldiers said he served throughout the war without carrying on a single intelligible conversation.

Another unusual fact about the Civil War concerned women. You read in a previous chapter about the contributions women made on the home front. In addition, more than 3,000 served as nurses in hospitals and at the battlefront, and an untold number even worked as spies. But these efforts were not all that unusual. What was unusual is that 400 women disguised themselves as men and fought as soldiers!

Two of the better-known women who posed as male soldiers were Loreta Velazquez and Sarah Edmonds. Velazquez fought in the Confederate Army and Edmonds in the Union.

Loreta Velazquez was the wife of an army officer stationed at Fort Leavenworth, Kansas, when the war began in 1861. Refusing to be separated from her husband when he marched off to fight for the Confederacy, Loreta thought of a way to join him. She cut her dark hair, glued on a false mustache and goatee, and overnight became Lieutenant Harry Buford of the Confederacy!

Velazquez's disguise fooled everyone. She practiced speaking in a deep voice and even mastered the art of spitting! Confident in her masquerade, she then recruited a company of male volunteers and marched off to be with her husband.

Her husband must have been quite surprised when "Lieutenant Buford" suddenly appeared in camp. Nevertheless, he went along with the deception and permitted her to serve as his aide. When he was killed in an accident shortly afterward, "Lieutenant Buford" kept her disguise and continued as a Confederate officer. Some sources say she was later appointed a temporary company commander at the First Battle of Bull Run. When her identify was finally discovered in 1863, she served out the remainder of the war as a spy.

Sarah Edmonds was a "tomboy" from Canada who had never enjoyed the life of a lady to begin with. She grew up hunting and fishing with her brothers

Frances Clalin, one of a number of women who disguised themselves as men and fought in the Civil War.

in Canada and was their equal at riding and shooting. When her parents arranged to have her marry someone she did not love, she ran away from home and disguised herself as a man. She first went to Connecticut and then to Michigan. She was working in Flint, Michigan, under the name of Franklin Thompson when the war began.

Edmonds enlisted in an infantry regiment as a male nurse. Her riding and shooting skills impressed her fellow recruits, but it was later as a Union spy that Sarah gained her reputation. She darkened her skin and went behind Confederate lines, posing as a slave assigned to perform chores for soldiers. In this role she supposedly obtained valuable information that she passed on to the Union. Her identity remained a secret throughout the war, and most of the soldiers with whom she served didn't learn she was a woman until many years after the war had ended.

The true identities of some women soldiers were never revealed. No one knows how many were killed in battle and buried undiscovered with their male counterparts. Others were identified only after being wounded. More than one Civil War surgeon was shocked to learn that the soldier on whom he was about to perform surgery was a woman.

Unusual facts about the Civil War are endless. As was pointed out at the beginning of this chapter, limited space permits the telling of only a few. But one or two more are worthy of note—and may be the strangest of all.

Ambrose Bierce, a journalist and writer who served in the Union Army, wrote after the war about the circumstances surrounding the death of a young Federal soldier. The soldier was found lying on his stomach, a musket ball imbedded in his side. When the musket ball was removed and examined, it was noted that it bore the name of the foundry that made it: Abbot. That, by a strange twist of fate, was also the name of the soldier whose life it ended.

If the above story is not strange enough for you, try this one: the Union Army numbered among its ranks a general named Jefferson Davis, and the Confederate Army had a private named Abraham Lincoln. Do you think both might have had to endure some good-natured teasing during their terms of service?

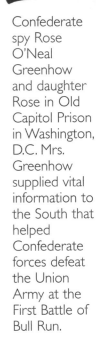

Confederate spy Rose O'Neal Greenhow and daughter Rose in Old Capitol Prison in Washington, D.C. Mrs. Greenhow supplied vital information to the South that helped Confederate forces defeat the Union Army at the First Battle of Bull Run.

Name _____ Date _____

Write a Persuasive Essay

In Chapter 8 you learned that there were many women who disguised themselves as men and fought as regular soldiers in the Civil War.

What is your opinion about women participating in combat? Should women be allowed or even expected to fight alongside men on the battlefield, or is the battlefield no place for a woman?

Choose one position or the other and write a persuasive essay on the lines provided. Give arguments supporting the way you feel.

From *Everyday Life: The Civil War* © 1999 Good Year Books.

Name _____ Date _____

Make False Statements True

All of these statements are false. Change the words in italics to make them true. Write the replacement words on the lines following the statements.

1. As many as *20 percent* of the soldiers who fought in the Civil War were under the age of sixteen. _____

2. The youngest general who served in the Civil War was *George Armstrong Custer.* _____

3. The cadets who fought at the Battle of New Market in 1864 were from the *United States Military Academy.* _____

4. Louis Philippe Albert d'Orleans and Eugene Ferdinand d'Orleans, two French royal princes, served on the staff of General *Ulysses S. Grant.* _____.

5. About *3,000* women disguised themselves as men and fought in the Civil War. _____

6. *Sarah Edmonds* enlisted in the Confederate Army to be with her husband. _____

7. Loreta Velazquez assumed the name *Franklin Thompson* when she marched off to war. _____

8. A *general* named Abraham Lincoln served in the Confederate Army. _____

9. A general named Jefferson Davis fought in the *Confederate* Army. _____

10. Ambrose Bierce was a well-known *photographer and cartoonist.* _____

11. *Few* foreigners in the armies of the North and the South served as common foot soldiers. _____

Name _____ Date _____

Complete a Vocabulary Exercise

Select the meaning of each word as it is used in Chapter 8. Circle the letter of the correct meaning. The paragraph in which each word appears in the narrative is written in parentheses.

1. **space** (paragraph 1)

   (a) distance

   (b) length of time

   (c) area or room

2. **slip** (paragraph 3)

   (a) pass without notice

   (b) slide

   (c) get away from

3. **lax** (paragraph 4)

   (a) not firm or tight

   (b) not strict

   (c) vague

4. **force** (paragraph 7)

   (a) power to control

   (b) a group of soldiers

   (c) strength

5. **conflict** (paragraph 8)

   (a) a fight or struggle

   (b) active opposition of people or idea

   (c) differ in thought or action

6. **title** (paragraph 10)

   (a) name showing rank or condition in life

   (b) championship

   (c) document showing ownership

7. **staff** (paragraph 10)

   (a) a stick or rod

   (b) group of officers assisting a commanding officer

   (c) group of employees

8. **front** (paragraph 13)

   (a) the first part

   (b) meet face to face

   (c) place where fighting is going on

9. **bore** (paragraph 22)

   (a) make a hole by means of a tool

   (b) a dull person

   (c) showed or displayed

From *Everyday Life: The Civil War* ©1999 Good Year Books.

Name _____ Date _____

Reading Between the Lines

When you draw conclusions from something you have read, you are "reading between the lines." You are comprehending ideas that are implied in a certain passage but not actually stated.

At right are several paragraphs about the life of Belle Boyd, a famous spy during the Civil War. After reading them, answer the questions at the bottom of the page on a separate sheet of paper.

A number of women served as spies during the Civil War. One of the most colorful was Belle Boyd.

Belle Boyd's war adventures began at the young age of seventeen when she shot and killed a Union soldier for raising a United States flag over her home in Martinsburg, Virginia. From there she went on to spying on Union troops stationed in Martinsburg. She relayed valuable information she attained to Confederate authorities in her own handwriting, and even signed her name at the bottom.

Belle was captured and imprisoned twice in Washington, D.C. She infuriated her guards by hanging a picture of Jefferson Davis in her cell and singing songs such as "Take Me Back to the Sunny South." Each time the guards entered to make her stop, she swept her cell after they left.

Belle romanced soldiers on both sides. Near the end of the war, she married a Yankee officer in London. Upon their return he was arrested as a Southern spy. He died shortly afterward, leaving Belle a widow at the age of twenty-one.

After the war, Belle toured the country, lecturing on her experiences. She was always aptly dressed, of course, in the uniform of a Confederate soldier.

1. What can you conclude from Belle Boyd's shooting and killing of a Union soldier when she was seventeen?

2. What is implied by Belle signing her name to the bottom of messages she sent to Confederate authorities?

3. What conclusion can be drawn from Belle's sweeping her cell each time Union guards departed?

African Americans in the War

When the Civil War began, free blacks and runaway slaves were not allowed to join the Union Army. They were employed as cooks, drivers, and scouts, but they were not accepted in the ranks as soldiers. Even after President Lincoln called for blacks to enlist in 1863, he meant for them to serve only as manual laborers.

Posters such as these encouraged black soldiers to enlist in the Union Army. This poster sought enlistees for what became the famous all-black 54th Massachusetts Regiment that fought so valiantly at Fort Wagner, South Carolina, in 1863.

Why this attitude toward African Americans? There were several reasons. First, President Lincoln feared offending the border states of Missouri, Maryland, Kentucky, and Delaware. These states supplied troops to both sides in the war, and Lincoln worried that accepting blacks into the Union Army would cause them to go over to the Confederacy.

A second reason why people in the North were so against African Americans in the military may surprise you. Even though the abolitionist movement was born in the North, abolitionists were ambiguous (not clear) in their feelings toward blacks. They hated slavery, but they did not look at African Americans as worthy of a higher status in life. Once slavery was ended, many people in the North felt that blacks should be content with menial jobs.

A third reason why African Americans were denied military service was the feeling that they would not make good soldiers. Even President Lincoln felt this way to a certain extent. He also believed that white officers would not want to command black troops.

Lincoln's Emancipation Proclamation on January 1, 1863, opened the doors to the military for African Americans. In the North alone, 186,000 blacks enlisted in the Union Army and another 30,000 in the Union navy. African Americans, in fact, made up 25 percent of the seamen in the Northern navy. In the South the Confederate Congress, desperately short of manpower, enlisted 300,000 slaves in 1865. But these recruits were slave-soldiers; they were not free men who joined of their own accord. The war ended before any of them were ever used.

Once accepted, African American soldiers suffered terrible discrimination in the Union Army. They were issued old, worn-out uniforms and weapons.

From *Everyday Life: The Civil War* ©1999 Good Year Books.

They received poor medical care and were always assigned the least appealing and most dangerous tasks. Finally, they were paid only $10 a month, in contrast to the $13 a white private received.

The inequality in pay led to a tragic incident in the all-black 3rd South Carolina Regiment in 1863. The 3rd South Carolina was one of the first black regiments in the Union Army, and its troops were a proud group. But when the Federal government failed to follow through on its promise to give them equal pay, a sergeant named William Walker took matters into his own hands. Walker ordered his company to stack their rifles outside the tent of their company commander. He then announced that their service of obligation had ended because the government had not fulfilled its obligation. Walker was immediately arrested, tried for insubordination, and executed.

Accounts vary as to the first African American regiment to actually be tested in battle. Most sources give the credit to the 54th Massachusetts, which was commanded by a white colonel named Robert Gould Shaw. The 54th led an assault on Fort Wagner, South Carolina, on July 18, 1863. Their bravery under fire changed a lot of opinions about blacks in combat.

When word spread that troops of black soldiers were being formed and that white officers were leading them, Confederate officials were enraged. They immediately sent orders to Southern forces in the field that all such white officers, if captured, were not to be treated as prisoners of war but executed on the spot.

The knowledge that they would be shot if captured did not deter Robert Gould Shaw and others. Shaw came from a distinguished Massachusetts family noted for its willingness to make sacrifices. His grandfather was a wealthy merchant who had fought in the Revolutionary War. His father was a kindhearted gentleman who gave away money generously to the poor and downtrodden. With such a background it is not surprising that twenty-six-year-old Robert Shaw volunteered to command the 54th Massachusetts Regiment.

Fort Wagner in South Carolina was important in that it defended Charleston Harbor. On July 10, 1863, Union General George C. Strong led an attack on the fort with two-and-a-half all-white regiments. He gained a foothold on the southern part of Morris Island, where Fort Wagner was

A black soldier holding a saber poses in his makeshift uniform. Almost 200,000 blacks served in the Union Army.

located, but lost 339 of his men in the process. The Confederates occupying the fort suffered only 12 casualties out of 1,200 defenders.

One week later, on the 18th, the Union brought in more cannon and mortar and bombarded the fort relentlessly. At dusk Federal troops staged another attack. This time they were led by the all-black 54th Massachusetts under the command of Colonel Shaw. With Shaw in front and shouting "Onward, men!" 650 African American soldiers moved steadily forward in the face of murderous fire. About 100 reached the gates of the fort, where they engaged in hand-to-hand fighting with the Rebels inside. Almost 300 were killed before their goal was attained. Included among the dead was Colonel Shaw.

Although Fort Wagner was not taken, the 54th Massachusetts displayed great courage under heavy fire. African American troops had been tested in battle and had not been found wanting. People in the North now began to think differently about blacks in the army.

Soldiers of the all-black 54th Massachusetts Regiment charge Fort Wagner in South Carolina on July 19, 1863. Their bravery impressed both Union and Confederate forces alike. From a lithograph by Kurz and Allison.

After Fort Wagner black regiments played prominent roles in a number of battles. They were instrumental at Petersburg and Richmond in Virginia and in Sherman's March to the Sea. And several regiments had the distinction of fighting in the last battle of the war. On April 9, 1865, African American soldiers participated in an attack on Fort Blakely at Mobile, Alabama. On that same day Lee surrendered to Grant at Appomattox Court House in Virginia.

White officers who commanded black troops were not alone in being singled out for mistreatment if captured. So were the troops themselves. One known massacre of African American soldiers actually occurred on April 12, 1864. The site was Fort Pillow, a Union fort on the Mississippi River in Tennessee. The Confederate officer blamed for the massacre was General

From *Everyday Life: The Civil War* ©1999 Good Year Books.

Nathan Bedford Forrest, who, after the war ended, helped found the Ku Klux Klan.

Fort Pillow was defended by a small force of 295 white and 262 black troops. The fort was important in protecting Union ships navigating the Mississippi. On the afternoon of April 12, approximately 1,500 Confederate troops attacked and easily overran the fort's defenders.

The army band of the 107th U.S. Colored Infantry poses for a picture at Fort Corcoran, Virginia.

Two versions of what followed exist. Confederate accounts state that the black soldiers were killed stubbornly defending the fort. A Union committee investigating the incident maintained that the blacks surrendered and then were massacred by the Confederates entering the gates. Rebel soldiers were said to have shouted, "No quarter! Shoot them down!" as they shot and bayoneted the helpless defenders. Among those killed were two women and three small children. Although the two reports naturally conflict, all evidence appeared to indicate that the Northern version of what happened was the true one.

The battles in which African American soldiers participated are too numerous to list. There were at least forty during the two years of the war in which black troops were involved. Regardless of the number, African Americans fought bravely. Twenty-one received the Congressional Medal of Honor, our nation's highest award for bravery. The medal is given only to service personnel who display "gallantry above and beyond the call of duty."

Numbers vary as to how many African American servicemen gave their lives on the field of battle. One account of the war written in 1898 lists only 2,751. More recent studies put the number of black soldiers and sailors killed at 68,000. The latter statistics may be more accurate. The author of the 1898 account surely was limited in the number of resources available to him at the time.

The Civil War changed the way many people thought about African Americans. It also changed the way African Americans thought about themselves. Many, because they had fought to end slavery and had distinguished themselves on the battlefield, began to think of themselves for the first time as Americans.

Name _____ Date _____

Solve Some Word Problems

Solve these word problems about African Americans who fought in the Civil War. Space is provided for you to work each problem.

Check your math book for a quick review of the terms used, if necessary.

1. Approximately 30,000 African Americans served in the Union Navy. If they made up 25 percent of the navy's total strength, how many men in all served in that branch of the Federal service?

   _____ men

2. Almost 2,500,000 troops served in the Union Army during the Civil War. About 186,000 of these were African Americans. What percentage of the total number of soldiers were African American?

   _____ %

3. Seven young African Americans enlisted in the Union Army shortly after the Emancipation Proclamation. James was 18, Robert 19, William 18, Jesse 20, Charles 21, David 25, and Ethan 26. With their ages in mind, answer the questions below.
   Which age represents the mode? _____
   The median? _____
   What is the range? _____
   The mean? _____

From *Everyday Life: The Civil War* ©1999 Good Year Books.

Name _____ Date _____

Recall Information You Have Read

Without looking back over the chapter, write your best answers to these questions.

1. What were several reasons why many people objected to African Americans serving as soldiers?

   _____

   _____

   _____

2. In what ways were African American soldiers victims of discrimination?

   _____

   _____

   _____

3. What was the South's reaction to the Union's use of African American troops?

   _____

   _____

   _____

4. Describe the role played by the all-black 54th Massachusetts Regiment at Fort Wagner in South Carolina.

   _____

   _____

   _____

5. Cite proof that African American soldiers fought bravely in the war.

   _____

   _____

   _____

Name _____ Date _____

Distinguish Between Fact and Opinion

Some of these statements concerning African Americans in the military are true. Others are false. On the line to the right of each, write **F** if the statement is a fact or **O** if the statement is an opinion.

1. President Lincoln at first intended for black enlistees in the Union Army to perform only manual labor. _____

2. Northern abolitionists in general supported African Americans in their desire to serve in the Union Army. _____

3. Ex-slaves who were accepted into the Union Army hated and despised their former masters. _____

4. Many people felt that white officers would refuse to serve with African American troops. _____

5. African American soldiers were happy serving in the Union Army. _____

6. The 54th Massachusetts Regiment was the most courageous of the all-black regiments that fought in the war. _____

7. Twenty-one African Americans received the Congressional Medal of Honor at war's end. _____

8. White officers who commanded African American troops faced the danger of being executed if captured. _____

9. Most Southerners approved of the Confederate massacre of black troops at Fort Pillow. _____

10. African American soldiers in the Union Army received less pay than white soldiers. _____

11. African American troops fought poorly compared to their white counterparts. _____

12. Had President Lincoln agreed to admit African Americans into the Union Army at the beginning of the war, the border states would have seceded and joined the Confederacy. _____

13. African American soldiers fought well in the attack on Fort Wagner, South Carolina. _____

From *Everyday Life: The Civil War* ©1999 Good Year Books.

Name _____ Date _____

Write a Letter

Before going into battle, soldiers experience many emotions: fear, anxiety, worry, doubt—possibly even excitement. The men of the 54th Massachusetts Regiment were no different. But the soldiers of the 54th probably had an additional concern on their minds. Since they were the first African American troops to see action, they had to cope with feelings that white soldiers had never experienced.

On the lines provided, compose a letter that an African American soldier might have written to a friend or loved one prior to the attack on Fort Wagner, South Carolina.

Date_____

Dear _____,

_____
_____
_____
_____
_____
_____
_____
_____
_____
_____
_____
_____
_____
_____
_____
_____
_____

Sincerely,

_____

CHAPTER 10

Hospitals and Prisons

This famous Winslow Homer lithograph depicts a nurse writing a letter for a wounded soldier.

You may have heard of Louisa May Alcott. In 1868, she published *Little Women,* one of the most popular books ever written. But before Louisa became a famous author, she served as a nurse for a short time during the Civil War.

Louisa May Alcott was shocked when she reported for duty at the Union Army Hospital in Washington, D.C. (Well, to call it a hospital was stretching things a bit, but it was the best the government had to offer at the time.) The site was the old Union Hotel, which was in a rotten and dilapidated condition. Louisa met with foul odors and even fouler surgeons and orderlies.

In the early months of the war, army surgeons resented the presence of women in what they considered male territory. Consequently, women nurses were confronted with scorn and complete lack of cooperation. Surgeons and orderlies went out of their way to make their lives as miserable as possible. But most of these women survived all such slights and insults, and by the end of the war their services were indispensable.

Army hospitals left much to be desired. Especially dreadful were the field hospitals. At best, a field hospital might be set up in an old abandoned building near the site of battle, but usually a field hospital consisted of a number of white tents pitched in a row in a field. In bad weather doctors and nurses waded through mud to reach patients. One nurse reported having to fish her shoes out of the mud with an umbrella handle before even proceeding to the tents of the wounded.

Medicines and supplies in hospitals were woefully inadequate. Antiseptics and antibiotics were not yet in use, and many patients who might have otherwise survived died of infection. Amputation was the common procedure for dealing with badly wounded limbs. At least 15 percent of hospitalized soldiers in the Civil War died from their wounds.

Dorothea Dix worked tirelessly to improve the way the mentally ill in the United States were treated.

Conditions might have been even worse were it not for the efforts of Dorothea Dix. Before the war Miss Dix had worked to improve conditions in the nation's prisons and mental hospitals. Shortly after Fort Sumter, she was appointed Superintendent of Women Nurses for the Union Army. Although she was in constant conflict with army surgeons, she managed to create a

From *Everyday Life: The Civil War* ©1999 Good Year Books.

corps (an organized and trained group) of dedicated nurses who served well throughout the war.

Miss Dix was a stern lady who was unpopular even with her nurses. Her process for screening applicants included eliminating those who wore jewelry and hoop skirts. Such women, she believed, might be interested more in romance than in caring for the wounded. Applicants also had to be above the age of thirty. Miss Dix's strict requirements undoubtedly turned away many younger women who might have made excellent nurses.

Another nurse who made her presence felt was Mary Ann Bickerdyke. After becoming head of a Union hospital in Illinois, she discovered that much of the food and clothing sent to wounded soldiers was being confiscated by dishonest surgeons and orderlies. So Mary Ann Bickerdyke came up with a plan. In a shipment of peaches intended for the wounded, she secretly put medicine designed to make patients vomit. After a short wait, the guilty parties exposed themselves by their moaning and nauseated condition. Miss Bickerdyke severely scolded the thieves and warned them that the next time she might use rat poison!

Clara Barton was one nurse who took matters into her own hands. She often showed up on battlefields driving a wagon filled with food and medical supplies. She worked in areas so close to where fighting was taking place that a bullet once passed through her sleeve and killed a soldier she was tending. As previously mentioned, Clara Barton later founded the American Red Cross.

Mary Walker was a physician—an unusual profession for women of her time—who served as a surgeon for the Union Army. She was captured while in service and imprisoned for several months. Later she was the only woman to receive the Medal of Honor, the highest military award given by the United States government.

The Confederacy was slow to use women as nurses. Southern gentlemen considered their ladies far too delicate for such a task. Still, women like Kate Cummings recruited thousands of nurses to work in military hospitals. And Sally Tompkins of Richmond established a twenty-two-bed hospital in the home of a friend. Her enthusiasm and efforts brought praise from none other than Jefferson Davis himself.

Women on both sides did more than give medicine, serve food, and wash feverish faces. They also doubled as cooks and

Clara Barton, a nurse who regularly risked her life to help the wounded on the battlefield. She later founded the American Red Cross. From a photograph by Mathew Brady.

letter writers. Many discovered that a major part of their job consisted in simply being a good listener and offering words of comfort when needed.

Wounded Confederate soldiers relax on Marye's Heights after a smashing victory over Union forces at the Battle of Fredericksburg in Virginia, December 1862.

As shocking as the state of military hospitals were, conditions in military prisons were even worse. Inhumane treatment and indescribable suffering characterized prisons in both the North and the South. There was, however, no deliberate plan on the part of either government that prisons should be so. In both armies, soldiers were often underfed and seldom able to receive proper medical attention. It only follows that the lack of sufficient food and medical supplies would be worse in the prison camps.

During the four years of the war, Federal troops took 215,000 Confederate soldiers prisoner. Some were released when they swore a loyalty oath to the Union. The Confederates in turn captured some 211,000 Union troops and marched them off to prison camps.

The Civil War was the first American war that saw prisoners taken in such large numbers. As a result, neither side was prepared to deal with the problem that faced them. At first there were genuine efforts to work out a suitable plan for prisoner exchange. But as the war wore on, misunderstandings and ill will caused talks to break down, and few prisoners were ever actually exchanged.

More than 150 places were used as prisons on both sides. Sometimes a prison consisted of an abandoned building or warehouse. Sometimes it might be an old penitentiary or even a ship. Often, prisons consisted of hastily constructed clapboard buildings with dirt floors. At Andersonville, Georgia, many of the 46,000 Federal prisoners lived in the open with no protection whatsoever against the heat or cold.

Several prisons in both the North and the South were notorious for the high number of deaths that occurred within their walls and fences. Union prison camps at Elmira, New York, and at Camp Douglas and Rock Island in Illinois were in many ways just as deplorable as the Confederate prison at Andersonville, which undeniably was the worst of them all. Elmira existed for only a year, yet 2,963 of the 12,123 Confederate prisoners held there died. At

From *Everyday Life: The Civil War* ©1999 Good Year Books.

Rock Island, 1,960 Confederate prisoners out of 12,400 died in the twenty months the camp was in operation.

The South operated several infamous camps, one of which was Libby Prison in Richmond. But none could compare with Andersonville. Andersonville was situated on twenty-seven acres in southwestern Georgia. It was basically a camp of tents, but conditions were so overcrowded that many of the prisoners, as mentioned above, lived and slept in the open. A Confederate surgeon sent by the government in Richmond to inspect the camp was shocked by what he found. Dysentery, scurvy, and gangrene took more than a hundred lives a day. Exposure and starvation caused more deaths. No attention was paid to hygiene, and a stream that ran through the middle of the camp was so polluted that men died of blood poisoning after getting a simple scratch or insect bite.

An emaciated (extremely thin) Union prisoner from the Andersonville prison is exchanged at Vicksburg, MIssissippi, in 1865. Henry Wirz, the commandant of Andersonville, was tried and executed after the war for ignoring the deplorable conditions that existed in his camp.

Andersonville was in operation for only nine months. But during that time, 12,900 of the 46,000 Union prisoners held there died. After the war, the prison's commandant, Henry Wirz, was executed by the Federal government for neglecting the atrocious conditions at the camp.

Toward the end of the war, Washington and Richmond worked out a deal to exchange prisoners who were too ill to fight but well enough to travel. But even these plans resulted in more inhumane treatment and deaths. At Elmira Prison 1,200 gravely ill Confederate prisoners were sent by train from Elmira to Baltimore. No doctors or nurses accompanied them, which meant they received no medical attention along the way. At Baltimore they were to be loaded onto a steamship for the final leg of the journey South. When the train arrived at Baltimore, however, Federal doctors discovered that five of the prisoners had died en route. Sixty others were rushed to Baltimore hospitals to save their lives.

By the end of the war, 25,976 Confederate soldiers and 30,218 Union soldiers had died in prison camps. The horrid conditions endured by these unfortunate men during their imprisonment had caused concerned citizens in both the North and the South to write letters to their governments asking them to intervene.

But not all citizens. At some camps curious passersby had no such feelings of concern for the wretched conditions under which the prisoners lived. Instead, they paid modest fees for the privilege of climbing observation towers and gawking at the poor souls inside the fences!

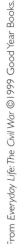

From *Everyday Life: The Civil War* ©1999 Good Year Books.

Name _____ Date _____

Prepare a Time-Machine Journal

Imagine that a time machine has whisked you back to an army hospital in the year 1863. Compose a journal describing your experiences. In your journal include the following:

1. The pitiable state of medical knowledge characteristic of the time

2. What you would tell doctors and nurses about modern hospitals and medical procedures

Dear Journal,
_____
_____
_____
_____
_____
_____
_____
_____
_____
_____
_____
_____
_____
_____
_____
_____
_____
_____

Name _____ Date _____

Conduct an Interview

Imagine that you are a Civil War-era reporter sent to interview a doctor with rather strong opinions about women being introduced into the nursing ranks. The doctor you have been assigned to interview has recently been forced to accept women as nurses in his army hospital in Washington. Because these are male-dominated times, the doctor is understandably quite miffed.

Write how you think the doctor might have responded to the questions at right. Any question answered "yes" or "no" should be followed with an explanation.

1. "Doctor, why are you so opposed to women serving as nurses?"

   _____

   _____

   _____

2. "Doctor, why do you think the nursing profession should be limited to men?"

   _____

   _____

   _____

3. "Doctor, how well do you think your new women nurses will hold up to the stress of daily having to deal with horribly wounded men?"

   _____

   _____

4. "Doctor, do you consider yourself prejudiced against women?"

   _____

   _____

   _____

5. "Doctor, should these women prove your opinions to be wrong, will you publicly offer your apologies to them?"

   _____

   _____

   _____

   _____

Name _____ Date _____

Hospital and Prison Puzzle

Across

3 _____ Tompkins, Confederate nurse

5 Camp Douglas was in this state.

8 Where Andersonville was

10 _____ Cummings, Confederate nurse.

12 Last name of the founder of the Red Cross

13 Minimum age to be one of Dorothea Dix's nurses

14 Dorothea Dix was the first Superintendent of _____.

Down

1 _____ Ann Bickerdyke

2 President Jefferson _____

4 Confederate prison in Richmond

6 First name of author of *Little Women*

7 Commandant at Andersonville

9 Union prison in New York

11 Common field hospital "buildings"

From *Everyday Life: The Civil War* ©1999 Good Year Books.

This reward poster appeared five days after Lincoln died. His murderer, John Wilkes Booth, was trapped and killed two weeks later in a barn near Bowling Green, Virginia.

to the sea" during the latter months of 1864. Almost nothing could be seen but gutted factories and homes with little more standing than chimneys. The completeness of the destruction in some areas was mind-boggling.

Travelers who toured the South immediately after the war told similar stories of the ruin and desolation. In many places nothing remained. Houses, crops, fences, cows, horses, pigs—all were gone. Confederate soldiers returning home had little on which to build a new life. Often, they had nothing to eat. Even ex-Confederate generals went about seeking any kind of work that would allow them to feed their families.

Why, you might ask, did people not just go to the nearest general store and buy what they needed? Certainly some people had stashed away considerable sums in the event of such hard times. The answer is that Confederate money after the war was practically worthless. The prices of foodstuffs and other needed items were simply out of the reach of many. With nothing to eat, widows and orphans who had been reduced to begging filled the streets of Southern towns. Federal relief commissions set up shortly after the fighting surely prevented these victims of the war from starving to death.

Without money or credit, planters had no way to recover their losses. They could not borrow money to put in crops or to pay hired hands. As a result, many planters were forced to divide their holdings just to survive. Others made do as best they could. One visitor to a South Carolina community reported seeing an ex-planter sitting in the corner of what once had been his magnificent estate. All he had left was a shell of his former lovely home. What was the planter doing? He was supporting himself by selling tea and molasses to any of his former slaves who happened to pass by.

Southerners reacted to the end of the war in different ways. Many welcomed Lee's surrender and the peace that it brought. Lee himself even stated that it was time to put the past behind and cooperate with the North in restoring the South to its feet.

Although there were no guerrilla activities or "last stands" by diehard Rebels, there was a lot of resentment and hatred on the part of some individuals. Many Southerners were bitter because they found themselves poverty-stricken after the fighting ceased. They had lost everything, and they would blame the Yankees (a commonly used slang term for Northerners) for many years to come for their desperate plight. Hate seemed to be the one thing that kept some of them going. One ex-hotel owner who found himself penniless told a reporter that he lived only to hate the North. He stated that

From Everyday Life: The Civil War ©1999 Good Year Books.

he got up at 4:30 each morning and stayed awake until past midnight "just to hate Yankees!"

Other factors added to the bitterness. The Radical Republican Congress passed laws spelling out what the eleven Confederate states had to do to be readmitted to the Union. Southerners resented these laws. One required that each state had to draw up a new constitution subject to Congress's approval. Another stated that before being readmitted, a state had to ratify the Fourteenth Amendment granting full citizenship to all African Americans. Still another forbade all former Confederate officials from holding public office.

All that remained of Charleston, South Carolina, after Union artillery bombarded the city.

But perhaps the most difficult pill for many Southerners to swallow was military occupation. The South was divided into five military districts, and Federal troops remained on Southern soil until 1877. During this time, state legislatures came under the control of scalawags, carpetbaggers, and ex-slaves.

Scalawags were Southerners who cooperated fully with Federal authorities. Most were wealthy planters and businessmen. Carpetbaggers, so-called because their traveling bags were made of carpet, were Northerners who came South for personal gain. Some came because they were reformers truly interested in racial justice. Others came simply for loot—to take advantage of a beaten enemy. But most came to attain political power and the rewards associated with it.

In spite of their plight, most Southerners accepted the changes thrust upon them and tried to go on with their lives. But many did not. In 1866 the Ku Klux Klan was organized in Pulaski, Tennessee. At first the Klan was intended to be only a social organization of Confederate war veterans. But it soon grew into a radical association that used terror tactics to keep African Americans from voting or running for office. Through threats, beatings, and lynchings, it accomplished its goal. By the end of the Reconstruction era in 1877, whites had regained control of state legislatures.

No sooner had Federal troops left the South than whites began to pass laws to keep African Americans out of politics. These laws, called Black Codes, established such voting requirements as literacy tests and a poll tax. Since most blacks could not read and few had money, the laws prevented them from exercising the rights guaranteed them by the Fourteenth and Fifteenth Amendments.

From *Everyday Life: The Civil War* ©1999 Good Year Books.

"When Johnny
Comes
Marching
Home" was
one of a
number of
popular songs
of the Civil
War. Others
included
"Dixie,"
"Tenting on
the Old Camp
Ground," and
"The Battle
Hymn of the
Republic."

And what about the four million slaves whom the Civil War had set free? Nearly all were uneducated and owned no property. What would they do? With no other means of support, many went to work for their former masters as sharecroppers. (Sharecroppers are farmers who turn over part of what they grow to their landlords in return for using parts of the landlord's land.) Others left to seek employment in the booming factories of the North. And some went west to Kansas and other areas to become homesteaders.

The Civil War did more than just do away with slavery and preserve the Union. From its wake emerged a stronger America. Prior to 1861 our nation was little more than a loose confederation of states. The federal government had almost no contact with the average citizen, who looked to local government to satisfy his or her needs. But after 1865 the government in Washington began to play a larger role in the daily lives of people. And, more importantly, the idea of secession died along with the Confederacy. The Civil War proved beyond doubt that no state had the right to withdraw from the Union.

Strangely enough, the bitterness and the wounds left by the war were in part healed by the soldiers themselves. Beginning in the 1870s, Union and Confederate veterans began holding joint reunions where they discussed and relived the conflict. They even began to return captured battle flags to the relatives of members of the regiments from which the flags came.

Today, the Civil War lives on in many ways. Countless pictures, statues, monuments, and parks remind us of those four terrible years in our nation's history. Also, reenactments of major battles regularly take place on both sides of the Mason-Dixon Line. And each year on the last Monday in May, we celebrate Memorial Day, which was originally established to honor all servicemen who died in the Civil War. (Memorial Day was later broadened to include service personnel who gave their lives in America's wars since that time.)

The Civil War also lives on in the many songs that Union and Confederate soldiers made popular. Some of the better known are "The Battle Hymn of the Republic," "Dixie," "The Yellow Rose of Texas," "Tenting on the Old Camp Ground," "When Johnny Comes Marching Home Again," and "Home Sweet Home."

The Civil War was unlike any other conflict in our long history. It is the only war in which American has fought American. We can only hope that the lessons learned from that experience will assure that it never happens again.

From *Everyday Life: The Civil War* ©1999 Good Year Books.

Name _____ Date _____

Write a Letter

Imagine yourself traveling through the South in the months immediately following the Civil War. Write a letter to a friend relating your experiences. Describe sights you have seen and people you have met.

Date _____

Dear _____,

_____

_____

_____

_____

_____

_____

_____

_____

_____

_____

_____

_____

_____

_____

_____

_____

_____

_____

Your friend,

_____

Name _____ Date _____

Solve an Aftermath Puzzle

Fill in the sentences at the bottom of the page to complete the puzzle dealing with the aftermath of the Civil War.

```
_ _ A _
  F _ _ _
_ _ _ _ _ T _ _ _ _ _
  _ _ E _ _ _
  _ _ R _ _ _
  _ _ M _
_ A _ _ _ _ _
  T _ _
_ _ _ _ H
```

1. The Ku Klux _____ terrorized ex-slaves into not voting.

2. After the Civil War, the South was divided into _____ military districts.

3. A _____ was a Northerner who went to the South for personal gain.

4. Federal troops occupied the South for _____ years.

5. _____ Johnson succeeded Abraham Lincoln as President.

6. "The Battle _____ of the Republic" was a popular song of the Civil War.

7. _____ Republicans controlled Congress in the years following the Civil War.

8. A poll _____ prevented most African Americans from voting in the post-Reconstruction South.

9. John Wilkes _____ assassinated Abraham Lincoln.

From *Everyday Life: The Civil War* ©1999 Good Year Books.

Name _____ Date _____

Complete Sentence or Fragment?

Can you distinguish between a complete sentence and a fragment? Fragments are statements that either lack a verb or a subject or do not express a complete thought. Fragments may be used in certain situations, but it is usually best to use complete sentences when writing.

At right is a group of statements relating to Chapter 11. Some items are fragments, while others are complete sentences. On the line to the left of each, write F if the statement is a fragment or S if it is a sentence. In the space below each statement that you mark as a fragment, rewrite the statement to make it a complete sentence.

1. After President Lincoln was assassinated. _____

_____

_____

2. More soldiers died in the Civil War from disease than from bullets. _____

_____

3. John Wilkes Booth, a Southern sympathizer. _____

_____

_____

4. When Federal troops left the South. _____

_____

5. While the North suffered only minimal damage from the war, parts of the South were devastated. _____

_____

6. Hunger was a major problem in the South after the Civil War. _____

_____

7. No sooner had Lincoln been assassinated. _____

_____

8. Many ex-slaves became sharecroppers after the war. _____

_____

9. "The Yellow Rose of Texas," a popular song of the Civil War. _____

_____

_____

Name _____ Date _____

Rewrite a Part of History

Suppose that John Wilkes Booth had failed in his attempt to assassinate President Lincoln on the night of April 14, 1865. Suppose that the President had lived and was able to carry out his proposed policy of leniency toward the South after the war.

How do you think history might have turned out differently if such a scenario had occurred? Would there have been the bitterness that lingered in the South for years? How might African Americans have fared? Would the Ku Klux Klan and other hate groups have arisen?

Write your thoughts on the lines.

From *Everyday Life: The Civil War*
©1999 Good Year Books.

Answers to Activities

Chapter 1

Name Those States and Territories

The Union States—California, Connecticut, Illinois, Indiana, Iowa, Kansas, Maine, Massachusetts, Michigan, Minnesota, New Hampshire, New Jersey, New York, Ohio, Oregon, Pennsylvania, Rhode Island, Vermont, Wisconsin

The Confederate States—Alabama, Arkansas, Florida, Georgia, Louisiana, Mississippi, North Carolina, South Carolina, Tennessee, Texas, Virginia

The Border States—Delaware, Kentucky, Maryland, Missouri

Territories That Fought for the Union — Colorado, Dakota, Nebraska, Nevada, New Mexico, Utah, Washington

Chapter 2

Reading Between the Lines

Answers will vary but should resemble the following:

1. The Union had a decided advantage and probably should have won the war.
2. The Confederacy had better leadership.
3. Southerners believed that Northern soldiers were inferior.
4. The U.S. Army was in no position to fight a war.
5. The South did not need to take the offensive.
6. Wars tended to drag on for a long time.
7. Families and relatives were divided in their loyalties.

Help Thomas Get to Minnesota

1. Arkansas, Missouri, Iowa
2. Little Rock, Jefferson City, Des Moines
3. Boston
4. Missouri
5. Northwest (or west northwest)
6. North
7. Wisconsin, Illinois, Nebraska, Dakota
8. St. Paul
9. North

Chapter 3

Use Context Clues to Complete Sentences

famous; acquired; unlikely; thin; suffering; attempted; deeply; unpopular; teased; stepped; inspired; encouraging; rally; amidst; stone

Solve Some Bull Run Word Problems

1. 6 mph   2. 6:30 p.m.   3. 45%
4. 4,480 casualties

Chapter 4

Solve a Leader Crossword Puzzle

Across: 2. rights   4. log   5. Honest
          8. Mississippi   10. War   12. farming
          13. cotton   14. Traveller

Down: 1. Union   3 horses   6. Ohio
        7. Virginia   9. Point   11. reading

Interpret Some Famous Quotes

Answers will vary but should resemble the following:

1st quote—A nation split over some issue will likely fall.

2nd quote—There is always some way to preserve the peace and avoid war.

3rd quote—We want to do as we please without interference from Washington.

4th quote—Everyone needs to work together and let bygones be bygones.

Name Those Leaders

1. Lincoln, Davis
2. Lee
3. Grant
4. Lee, Grant, Davis
5. Davis
6. Lee
7. Lincoln
8. Lee, Grant, Davis
9. Lincoln
10. Grant
11. Davis
12. Lincoln
13. Lee
14. Lincoln
15. Lincoln
16. Grant
17. Lee

Chapter 5

Put On Your Thinking Cap
Answers will vary but should resemble the following:

1. There was no way to check the ages of boys wanting to enlist (no Social Security cards, driver's licenses, etc.).
2. The two sides spoke the same language and shared a common knowledge of America. Also, many had family members and relatives fighting for the other side.
3. The tactic of advancing in neat lines or rows for the enemy to mow down.

Interpret a Pie Graph
1. 250,000   2. 1,750,000   3. 500,000

Chapter 6

Fill In a Venn Diagram
Answers will vary but should include some of the following:

The North
1. Some factory owners and farmers became wealthy.
2. Workers labored long hours for low pay.
3. There were draft riots.
4. Most people ate meat and potatoes at meals.

Both
1. Life was hard for the average family.
2. Women sewed, rolled bandages, and worked in hospitals.
3. People waited months and even years to learn the fate of loved ones.

The South
1. Hunger was a serious problem.
2. Children went barefoot in warm months to save leather.
3. Northern bummers raided farms.
4. Prices skyrocketed.
5. People used substitutes for food staples.
6. There were food riots in various cities.

Solve Some Home-Front Word Problems
1. a. $0.25   b. $17.10   c. $0.90
2. a. 4.4 months   b. 6¼ months
3. $22.50

Chapter 7

Solve an Innovations Puzzle
1. silk   2. *Monitor*   3. Barton   4. Lowe
5. Virginia   6. Brady   7. draft
8. Sanitary   9. Balloons   10. Manassas
11. musket

Use Context Clues to Complete Sentences
used; descending; some time; launched; event; town; height; later; passengers; safely; heroes; rewarded; place; flew; distance; landed; crashing; along

Improve Your Map Skills
1. channel; James, Nansemond, Elizabeth; Richmond; southeast
2. Tennessee, North Carolina; Nashville, Raleigh; West Virginia, Kentucky; Charleston, Frankfort.
3. Washington, Columbia; Potomac; Maryland
4. Blue Ridge, Allegheny

Chapter 8

Make False Statements True
1. 10%   2. Galusha Pennypacker
3. Virginia Military Institute
4. George McClellan   5. 400
6. Loreta Velazquez   7. Harry Buford
8. private   9. Union
10. journalist and writer   11. Most

Complete a Vocabulary Exercise
1. c   2. a   3. b   4. b   5. a   6. a
7. b   8. c   9. c

From *Everyday Life: The Civil War* ©1999 Good Year Books.

ANSWERS TO ACTIVITIES

Draw Conclusions from What You Have Read
Answers will vary but should resemble the following:
1. She was hotheaded, fearless, and staunchly Confederate.
2. She was bold and possibly arrogant.
3. She despised Union soldiers and held them in contempt.

Chapter 9

Solve Some Word Problems
1. 20,000   2. 7.44%
3. mode, 18; median, 20; range, 7; mean, 21

Reading Between the Lines
1. Lincoln feared the border states would join the Confederacy; some people thought blacks would not make good soldiers; some believed white officers might not command them
2. They received worn-out uniforms and weapons; got less pay; received poor medical attention; were given the most unappealing tasks and assignments.
3. The South was furious. Orders went out to execute white officers commanding African American troops.
4. The 54th led the charge on the fort, showing great bravery and losing almost half its strength, or number of soldiers.
5. Twenty-one African American soldiers received the Congressional Medal of Honor.

Distinguish Between Fact and Opinion
1. F   2. O   3. O   4. F   5. O   6. O
7. F   8. F   9. O   10. F   11. O
12. O   13. F

Chapter 10

Hospital and Prison Puzzle
Across: 3. Sally   5. Illinois   8. Georgia
10. Kate   12. Barton   13. thirty
14. Nurses
Down: 1. Mary   2. Davis   4. Libby
6. Louisa   7. Wirz   9. Elmira
11. tents

Chapter 11

Solve an Aftermath Puzzle
1. Klan   2. five   3. carpetbagger
4. twelve   5. Andrew   6. Hymn
7. Radical   8. tax   9. Booth

Complete Sentence or Fragment?
(Sentences that students rewrite from fragments will vary.)
1. F   2. S   3. F   4. F   5. S   6. S
7. F   8. S   9. F

Additional Resources

Books for Children

Angle, Paul. *A Pictorial History of the Civil War Years.* Garden City, New York: Doubleday & Company, 1967.

Biel, Timothy L. *The Civil War.* San Diego: Lucent Books, 1991.

Chang, Ina. *A Separate Battle: Women and the Civil War.* New York: Lodestar Books, 1991.

Kallen, Stuart. *A Nation Divided.* Edina, Minnesota: Abdo & Daughters, 1990.

Moore, Kay. *If You Had Lived at the Time of the Civil War.* New York: Scholastic, 1994.

Murphy, Jim. *The Boys' War.* New York: Clarion Books, 1990.

Books for Adults

Kent, Zachary. *The Civil War: A House Divided.* Hillside, New Jersey: Enslow Publishers, 1994.

Hansen, Joyce. *Between Two Fires: Black Soldiers in the Civil War.* New York: Franklin Watts, 1993.

Boatner, Mark M., III. *The Civil War Dictionary.* New York: David McKay Company, 1959.

Davis, Burke. *The Civil War: Strange & Fascinating Facts.* New York: Fairfax Press, 1982.

Canby, Courtlandt. *A History of Weaponry.* The New Illustrated Library of Science and Invention. London: Leisure Arts Limited Publishers, 1963.

Webb, Willard, ed. *Crucial Moments of the Civil War.* New York: Bonanza Books, 1961.

Price, William H. *The Civil War Handbook.* Fairfax, Virginia: L. B. Prince Co., 1961.

Robertson, James I., Jr. *The Civil War.* Washington, D.C.: U.S. Civil War Centennial Commission, 1963.

From *Everyday Life: The Civil War* ©1999 Good Year Books.